Following God

THE BOOK OF
Ephesians

THE BOOK OF
Ephesians

A Verse-By-Verse Bible Study
by

EDDIE RASNAKE

Advancing the Ministries of the Gospel

 **AMG** *Publishers*

God's Word to you is our highest calling.

CHATTANOOGA, TENNESSEE

The Book of Ephesians

© 2003 by Eddie Rasnake

Published by AMG Publishers. All Rights Reserved.
No part of this publication, including the artwork, may be reproduced, stored in a retrieval system, or transmitted in any form or by any means, electronic, mechanical, photocopying, recording, or otherwise—except for brief quotations in printed reviews, without the prior written permission of the publisher.

Fourth Printing, 2006

ISBN: 0-89957-319-3

Cover and text design by Denise Harris
at ImageWright Marketing and Design, Chattanooga, TN (www.imagewright.net)

Editing and layout by Rick Steele

Printed in the United States of America
11 10 09 08 07 06 –EB– 9 8 7 6 5 4

This book is dedicated to my grandparents:

Loetta and
the late Blake Cornett

As a child growing up in a broken home, their love and support filled an important gap in my life. As an adult, I continue to learn from and lean on the example they set in life.

Acknowledgments

This work goes forth to those who have been an encouragment in the publication of all the books in this series: *Life Principles from the Old Testament, Life Principles from the Women of the Bible* (Books 1 and 2), *Life Principles from the Prophets of the Old Testament, Life Principles from the New Testament Men of Faith,* and *Life Principles for Worship from the Tabernacle,* as well as *Living God's Will* and *First Steps for the New Christian.* Special thanks to my friends and co-laborers in the making of many of these books, Wayne Barber and Rick Shepherd. I am also especially grateful to my church friends at Woodland Park Baptist who have helped to shape so many of these studies. Thanks to all the good folks at AMG Publishers, expecially Rick Steele, Trevor Overcash, Dale Anderson, Warren Baker, and Dan Penwell. Most of all, I remain grateful to the Lord Jesus, who continues to teach me what it means to follow Him with a whole heart.

EDDIE RASNAKE

About the Author

Eddie Rasnake met Christ in 1976 as a freshman in college. He graduated with honors from East Tennessee State University in 1980. He and his wife, Michele, served for nearly seven years on the staff of Campus Crusade for Christ. Their first assignment was the University of Virginia, and while there they also started a Campus Crusade ministry at James Madison University. Eddie then served four years as campus director of the Campus Crusade ministry at the University of Tennessee. In 1989, Eddie left Campus Crusade to join Wayne Barber at Woodland Park Baptist Church as the Associate Pastor of Discipleship and Training. He has been ministering in Eastern Europe in the role of equipping local believers for more than a decade and has published materials in Albanian, German, Greek, Italian, Romanian, and Russian. Eddie serves on the boards of directors of the Center for Christian Leadership in Tirana, Albania, and the Bible Training Center in Eleuthera, Bahamas. He also serves as chaplain for the Chattanooga Lookouts (Cincinnati Reds AA affiliate) baseball team. Eddie and his wife Michele live in Chattanooga, Tennessee with their four children.

About the Following God Series

Three authors and fellow ministers, Wayne Barber, Eddie Rasnake, and Rick Shepherd, teamed up in 1998 to write a character-based Bible study for AMG Publishers. Their collaboration developed into the title, *Life Principles from the Old Testament*. Since 1998 these same authors and AMG Publishers have produced five more character-based studies—each consisting of twelve lessons geared around a five-day study of a particular Bible personality. More studies of this type are in the works. Two unique titles were added to the series in 2001: *Life Principles for Worship from the Tabernacle* and *Living God's Will*. These titles became the first Following God™ studies to be published in a topically-based format (rather than character-based). However, the interactive study format that readers have come to love remains constant with each new Following God™ release. As new titles are being planned, our focus remains the same: to provide excellent Bible study materials that point people to God's Word in ways that allow them to apply truths to their own lives. More information on this groundbreaking series can be found on the following web page:

www.amgpublishers.com

Preface

Years ago, I was privileged to be part of an amazing scene at our local airport. A family in our church was arriving from Bulgaria with a little three year old girl they had just adopted out of an orphanage in Sophia. Ironically, this little girl shared the same birthday as my wife. As I led in this group of friends and well-wishers in prayer, I reflected on how much this little girl's future would differ from her past. Adjustments would need to be made along the way. She had to learn a new language and new customs. But she left behind a crowded orphanage to come to a new home—with her own bedroom and two parents all to herself! One of the first challenges this new family had was at mealtimes. The little girl would gorge herself almost to the point of being sick, because she wasn't used to the abundance of food. But she adjusted. Today I am amazed at how American she seems. That over-crowded orphanage in Bulgaria is a distant memory. She has been blessed with so many blessings.

You and I have a lot in common with that little girl. We have been adopted into God's family. We have a new life with new resources. We have been blessed with every spiritual blessing in the heavenly places in Christ. But we have some adjusting to do. We have a new identity and we must learn to live in it. We cannot live in the old identity any longer. Adjusting to our new identity as followers of Christ is really what the book of Ephesians is all about. The apostle Paul spends the first three chapters telling us how blessed we are, and the last three telling us what to do about it.

We are rich indeed! Yet too many believers live like spiritual paupers, constantly trying to get something from Christ instead of realizing they already have all things in Christ. The goal of this study is to help you live a life consistent with your high position in Christ. I pray your study of Ephesians will be both a blessing and a challenge.

Yours and His,

Eddie Rasnake

EDDIE RASNAKE

Table of Contents

lesson **1**

Ephesians 1:1-3

BOOK OVERVIEW

LIVING OUT YOUR POSITION IN CHRIST

A dusty letter, written on faded, cracked parchment, in a language most don't understand, to people long forgotten living in a place no longer significant. As you ponder the relevance of this Bible study on Ephesians, perhaps you may be thinking, "What could this letter possibly have that would interest me?" Yet this two-thousand-year-old letter is just as relevant today as the day it was written. Its message is needed just as much. Its impact has not faded over the generations. Its value is beyond measure. This epistle was penned by one of the pillars of the Christian faith, and makes up part of your Bible. It is the book we call "Ephesians." If you lived in a persecuted country and it was the only part of the Bible you possessed, you would still be immeasurably rich and equipped to walk with God in victory!

In the weeks ahead, we will dive deeply into this treasure chest of spiritual jewels called "Ephesians." We will walk verse by verse through its chapters and become intimately acquainted with all its wealth. Henrietta Mears, the saintly servant of half a century ago that so profoundly impacted the field of Christian education, called this letter "the Holy of Holies" of Paul's writings. In 2 Corinthians 12:2, Paul speaks of being *"caught up to the third heaven"* and hearing inexpressible words. If those words are higher than those we find expressed in the book of Ephesians, they are marvelous indeed! Paul writes to a church he founded, and tells them of a mystery that has been hidden for ages, but, at long last, God has chosen for it to be revealed.

"In this epistle [of Ephesians] we enter the Holy of Holies in Paul's writings."

—Dr. Henrietta Mears

The epistle to the Ephesians is arguably the greatest revelation of truth that God has given to man.

The book of Ephesians shows us the great mystery of the Church—not that building with red brick and white columns, but the body of Christ—the visible manifestation of God on planet earth. As believers, we are each members of that sacred body of which Christ is the head. While on earth, God gave Jesus a physical body in which to serve and suffer. After His ascension, the Church was founded—God's gift of a spiritual body through which Christ could serve and suffer. As a body of believers, we the Church serve in much the same capacity as Jesus did as an individual during His earthly ministry. We are Christ's hands and feet; we are the representation of God to a world that doesn't know Him. This message is nowhere more clearly articulated than in this book we call Ephesians. In the days and weeks ahead we will study that book, phrase by phrase, verse by verse, paragraph by paragraph, and we will see how this ageless message is to be lived out today!

Ephesians 1:1-3

THE AUTHOR OF EPHESIANS

I believe it was when I was a college student that I first really appreciated the concept of personal mail. Away from home for the first time and with a post office box to call my own, every day I would come by to see if anything was there. On a wall of post office boxes, I came to be able to single out my box from a distance and spy immediately if a letter was to be found within. Any mail was a blessing. The most frivolous junk mail got a thorough reading. But the high point of all high points was a personal letter from someone I loved. Nothing made my day like a letter from home. I would tear into the envelope and quickly make my way to the end of the letter to see who wrote it.

Much of the New Testament is made up of letters sent from and to someone. Yet in these letters, as was the culture of the day, the name of who wrote it is not to be found at the end, but at the beginning (much more efficient to my way of thinking). We need to realize that the book of Ephesians is a letter written from someone and to someone. It doesn't exist in a vacuum. It falls in the context of a relationship. To really understand all that its pages hold, we need to learn what we can of the relationship behind the letter. We need to know all we can glean of its author and of his audience. Today we will begin consideration of the letter's author.

📖 Read Ephesians 1:1 and write all you learn about the author of this letter.

Paul is an apostle of Christ and it is because of God's will.

He considers faithful christians a already be Saints.

Only a small number of men and women throughout history can be identified immediately by only their first name. Mary the mother of Jesus, Michelangelo, Galileo, Napoleon—their lives were so impactful on the culture of their day that their first names suffice for them to be recognized. In recent times we have seen entertainment celebrities gain such name recognition: Elvis, Madonna, and Oprah to name a scant few. Indeed, the apostle Paul was known by his first name throughout his ministry on earth and has become known by many millions more throughout the centuries. Ephesians 1:1 identifies the author by his first name and gives a brief description of his position and influence. Paul is called *"an apostle of Christ Jesus by the will of God."* He was not a self-appointed leader, but one called by God to represent Him.

📖 Look at the verses listed below and write what you learn there about the apostle Paul's life before his conversion.

Acts 7:58

Was witness to, and supporter of, the stoning of Stephen

Acts 8:1–3

Saul had a great zeal for undermining the church which he viewed as a heresy. He wasn't content to tolerate them or simply badmouth and discourage its followers - he actively sought to disrupt the members from continuing their practices

Acts 9:1–2

Proactively sought to find Christians outside of Israel and bring them back to Jerusalem where the High Priest and Sanhedrin had the power to prosecute heresy and stone people. Couldn't have happened in Damascus

Paul's name was originally "Saul," and we are introduced to him at the stoning of Stephen. He is, at this time, a "young man"; this probably explains why he merely collected the robes of those actually carrying out executions by stoning. Very quickly, however, Saul steps to the forefront of the persecution of Christianity (8:1–3). Like many of the devout Jews in Israel, Saul believed that if Israel wasn't pure, Messiah wouldn't come. He saw this sect of believers in Jesus as a stain on Israel needing to be purged. That Saul was able to provide leadership in the task of persecuting Christians and the fact that he possessed letters of authority from the high priest to carry out these persecutions give us some sense of how prominent a position Paul held among the Pharisees. It was this relentless pursuit of terrorizing Christ's church that led Saul to the Damascus road—where he dramatically encountered Christ.

📖 Read the apostle's testimony in Acts 9:1–30 and summarize how he came to be involved in taking the gospel to Gentiles such as those in the city of Ephesus.

As Saul began to extend his influence of persecution beyond just in Jerusalem and Judea, Jesus makes a personal appearance to change and embolden him to speak truth. He begins where he is - Damascus

Put Yourself in Their Shoes

THE APOSTLE PAUL

The apostle Paul was probably born around A.D. 2 and met Christ around A.D. 35. He ministered throughout much of the Roman Empire until his martyrdom in A.D. 68. He wrote thirteen letters of the New Testament through which he continues to minister to millions of believers in Jesus Christ.

Did You Know?

PAUL'S EDUCATION

The apostle Paul was a student of Gamaliel (Acts 22:3, 5:34), one of the outstanding rabbis in Jewish history. At the time of Christ, there were two main rabbis, Gamaliel and Hillel. Gamaliel was the more conservative of the two. It is Gamaliel who advised caution as the Sanhedrin wanted to put Peter and John to death in Acts 5.

Saul was on his way to Damascus to persecute Christians, but, before he reached the city, he encountered Christ and was converted and called as a "chosen instrument" to take the gospel to the Gentile world. Then Saul came to use the Greek equivalent (Paul) to identify with the Gentiles to whom God had called him to minister (Acts 9:15).

Immediately after his conversion, Paul traveled to Arabia (Galatians 1:17), most likely for the purpose of devout study and meditation on the marvelous revelation that had been made to him. Three years later, he returned to Damascus and began to preach the gospel *"boldly in the name of Jesus"* (Acts 9:27), but persecution forced him to flee to Jerusalem (Acts 9:25–29; 2 Corinthians 11:33) and then to his hometown of Tarsus (Galatians 1:21), where he again disappeared for another three years. During this time, God began a great work at Antioch, and Barnabas (who first welcomed Paul into the fellowship of the "Mother Church" [Acts 9:26–28]), tracked Paul down and enlisted him to help lead the new church (Acts 11:19–26). This seems to be the point at which Paul devoted himself full-time to the ministry.

THE AUDIENCE OF EPHESIANS

A number of years ago, my family closed the books on the estate of my great-grandparents when they sold the family home in rural Virginia. In the process of distributing the assets, I was given the family Bible, being the lone preacher among the kinfolk. This antiquated Bible, torn and tattered by age and use, apparently has been in our family since the mid-nineteenth century. It contained a treasure trove of family history with many significant dates of births, marriages, and deaths. While I was thumbing through its pages, I came across a letter written during the Great Depression that had obviously been saved there because it was so valued. I was fascinated. My great-grandfather wrote it to his parents who had died long before I was born. As I read the letter, I caught glimpses of what their lives were like as they held down the family farm and wrestled with making ends meet. I sensed the love and connection it reflected. It became a catalyst for many interesting conversations with my grandmother as I sought to understand all that was being said.

In a sense, the book of Ephesians is much like that letter I found in the family Bible. Who received this letter we call "Ephesians"? What were these people like? Why did Paul write to them? To really appreciate all that is being said, we must learn something of the relationship they had and the times in which they lived. Today we want to focus on what we can learn about the audience of Ephesians.

📖 Verse 1 reads, *"To the saints who are at Ephesus, and who are faithful in Christ Jesus."* What do you think it means that they are "saints"?

They have entrusted their spiritual well-being to the Power of Christ instead of their own power of self-righteousness.

Paul identifies the Ephesians as "saints" nine times in this short letter (Ephesians 1:1, 15, 18; 2:19; 3:8, 18; 4:12; 5:3; 6:18). What did the Ephesians do to qualify them as saints? Were they some kind of "super Christians" and thus entitled to special blessing? Here it is useful to go back to the original language. There is quite a discrepancy between the English word "saint" and the Greek word translated "saint." The Greek word for saint (*hágios*) doesn't refer to an elite group of "super Christians" but is one of the many New Testament terms used to describe one who has trusted Christ as Savior. The word means "one who has been set apart" and is related to the word "sanctified." Sanctification, or "setting apart" is the process God takes each believer through as He makes that believer more like Christ (Philippians 1:6).

📖 Read through Acts 18:18—19:10 and identify how the church at Ephesus was first started.

> Paul stopped there on the way to Macedonia and encountered those who were interested in the Gospel. However, he felt called to continue on. Priscilla & Aquilla arrived to help Apollos minister to the interested people. Paul returned a few years later to follow up on his desire to help them.

While ministering at Antioch, Paul and Barnabas were called by God to take the gospel to the rest of the Gentile world (Acts 13:2). It was on the second missionary journey that Paul first visited Ephesus briefly about A.D. 53 (Acts 18:19–21). The city was next ministered to by Apollos, a devout Jew who had been impacted by the ministry of John the Baptist. Though Apollos didn't fully understand the doctrines of Christ, he was a believer in Jesus, and apparently it was while he was visiting Ephesus that Priscilla and Aquilla came alongside him and clarified the doctrines of *"the way of God"* (Acts 18:26). About two years later, while on his third journey, Paul stayed in Ephesus for at least two years and preached the gospel throughout the entire area (Acts 19:1–20). During this time, he founded the Ephesian church. It was about nine years later, or A.D. 62, when Paul wrote to his children in the faith at Ephesus. Paul was then imprisoned in Rome (Ephesians 3:1; 4:1; 6:20), and he wanted to exhort these believers to *"walk in a manner worthy"* of the Lord (Ephesians 4:1). Although Paul was imprisoned and didn't know if he would live or die, as an *"apostle by the will of God"* (one sent with a commission), he had an obligation to teach the Ephesians and others God's truth and to build them in faith (Ephesians 4:11–12).

📖 Look at Acts 19:11–20 and summarize the evidences you see there of God's working at Ephesus.

> God's power, as demonstrated through Paul was widely evident. So much so, that some coveted the same and attention given him and desired to get their own commendation on his coat tails. The evil spirits were even aware of Paul.

The citizens of Ephesus were witnesses of the power of God to an extraordinary degree. Acts 19:11 tells us this. The sick were healed. Evil spirits were banished. Lives were being changed. The name of Jesus was being magnified. The fact that occult magic and demon possession were so widespread in Ephesus is indicative of the city's spiritual climate. Yet we also know that the working of God (acts of confession and repentance) was so

Did You Know?

THE CITY OF EPHESUS

During the reign of Rome, Ephesus was called "the first and greatest metropolis of Asia." The city was home to the temple of Diana (a heathen idol), which was recognized as one of the seven wonders of the world. Located on the Aegean Sea in what is now western Turkey, Ephesus was a commercial, political, and religious center of the day.

Did You Know?

TARGET READERSHIP

Some have argued that the book of Ephesians was written not to a specific church in Ephesus, but was a cyclical letter passed around from church to church. While we cannot conclude this for certain, there is some reason for such an idea. It lacks the customary names and personal greetings found in Paul's other letters. And we are told in Acts 19:10 that using Ephesus as his home base, Paul was instrumental in all who lived in the region of Asia hearing the word of the Lord. In addition, some good Greek manuscripts omit the words "at Ephesus" in 1:1 (though this could also be seen as evidence that it was originally written to Ephesus, and then later became a cyclical letter because of its valued content).

widespread in Ephesus (see verses 18–19) that the fruits of repentance were being manifest in the burning of pagan books valued at fifty thousand pieces of silver. Verse 20 of Acts 19 provides us with a fitting summary of the workings of God at Ephesus: *"So the word of the Lord was growing mightily and prevailing."*

Ephesians 1:1–3

DAY THREE

THE AIM OF EPHESIANS

Why did Paul write to the Ephesians? Was it just that the first of the month had rolled around and he had to get a newsletter out to his ministry partners? Was it simply that he had time on his hands, or that he needed something from them? To fully appreciate these books we call epistles, it is helpful to have some sense of why they were written. Today we want to focus on identifying the aim of the book of Ephesians.

We know from Ephesians 3:1 that Paul was in prison when he wrote this letter. It was probably written around A.D. 61, during his first Roman imprisonment. From his confinement, he penned this and other letters to the churches at Ephesus, Philippi, and Colosse, and to a man by the name of Philemon. Each of these letters has been recognized as carrying the weight of Scripture. More than any other reason, it would appear that Paul wrote these letters to continue his spiritual investments in the lives of those believers he was instrumental in establishing in the faith. But more than that, he obviously had some specific goals in mind—messages he wanted his readers to understand and be reminded of. Today we will look at these.

📖 Read Ephesians 1:3 and write down what you learn about the message of this book.

That Christ is the source and the means of all spiritual blessings.
_____
_____
_____

In Ephesians 1:3 Paul writes, *"Blessed be the God and Father of our Lord Jesus Christ, who has blessed us with every spiritual blessing in the heavenly places in Christ."* This is a fitting summary of all he will tell us in the pages ahead. He communicates here that the meat of the book is showing us what a tremendous wealth we have "in Christ." The Ephesians lived in a city of great commercial wealth and Paul wanted them to understand what real wealth is, where to find it, and what to do with it.

All the tremendous wealth we have *"in Christ"* has been given to us by God the Father, who only gives good gifts (James 1:17). When we are adopted into God's family, we become *"joint heirs"* with Christ (Romans 8:17 NKJV) and share in His inheritance (Ephesians 1:11–12; 1 Peter 1:1–4). What an awesome blessing it is to say that the One who has so richly blessed us Himself deserves to be blessed. (When applied to God, the word "blessed" means to adore and thank Him for all benefits). What more fitting response can we give?

📖 Ephesians 1:3 tells us that we have all these spiritual blessings *"in Christ."* In other words, He is where we find these blessings. Using a concordance, look up every time the term *"in Christ"* or *"in Him"* appears in Ephesians.

How many times does *"in Christ"* or *"in Him"* appear?

20

_____

What chapters contain most of these references?

1-3   .

_____

The realm of our spiritual blessings is *"in Christ."* That phrase and the related phrase, "in Him," is used some twenty times in the book of Ephesians (twenty-two if you include the phrase, *"in whom,"* which conveys the same idea [see 2:22 and 3:12]). Of those uses, all but two appear in the first three chapters. This is to be expected since these chapters focus primarily on "positional truth," those things that are true of us because we are His. Because we are "in Christ," we are able to draw on His wealth and resources.

📖 Read through Ephesians 4:1 and write your thoughts on how Paul wants us to act on what he has told us in the first three chapters.

He wants to make sure that everything we do is a reflection as much as possible of the glorious nature of God. Now that we have become such an integrated part of His purpose, dwelling and riches, there is simply no room for attitudes and behaviors that don't reflect his glory.

Chapter four marks a major division in Paul's thoughts in Ephesians. Up until this point, the whole focus has been on positional truth. In Ephesians 4:1, Paul transitions with the conjunctive adverb, *"therefore,"* and begins to put the emphasis on what we are to do because of our position. In this verse, Paul exhorts us to "walk" in a manner worthy of our calling or position. Paul uses the term "walk," six times throughout the next two chapters. Our position in Christ moves us to the practice of a worthy walk.

📖 Look at Ephesians 6:10–24 and record every time the command *"stand firm"* appears. Jot down your observations on what this command means.

That we can expect God's power to keep us in his presence no matter what comes. Our faith in his power is what enables our firmness in our standing.

_____

_____

_____

_____

Doctrine
SIT, WALK, STAND!

The great Chinese writer and preacher, Watchman Nee authored a commentary on the book of Ephesians entitled *Sit, Walk, Stand.* The creative title is taken from the three key words of that epistle describing the believer's position in Christ (seated with Him [chapters 1—3]), the believer's life in the world (walk worthy [4:1—6:9]), and the believer's attitude to the wiles of Satan (stand firm [6:10–24]). The title and outline of Watchman Nee's commentary give us a good working outline of the epistle to the Ephesians.

Word Study
STAND

The Greek word *histēmi* means "to stand before" or "to stand in front of or in the face of." *Histēmi* appears four times in Ephesians 6:10–18. Three of these appearances are reflected in the English word, "stand" (6:11, 13–14), and the fourth (accompanied by the prefix *"anti"* [against]) is translated "resist" (6:13). The most important thing in spiritual warfare is to keep standing.

Three times in these fifteen verses Paul exhorts us to *"stand firm"*! The context of this command is in relation to the spiritual battle we encounter with Satan, our enemy. Standing in our position in Christ is not only central to walking worthy, but also to standing our ground against the attacks of the enemy. Notice, we are not called to chase Satan, but rather, to stand our ground and not allow Satan to move us.

Ephesians 1:1-3

DAY FOUR

THE ADMONITION OF THE EPHESIAN EXAMPLE

Ephesus was a pagan place with much evil. The fact that the power of God penetrated this sin-stained city ought to encourage us all. How far this early church came is evidenced by the many times we see it mentioned elsewhere in the New Testament. Apparently, the church was first initiated via Paul's brief visit, Priscilla and Aquilla's ongoing presence, and even the sowing of Apollos. Paul's later visit and three-year stay helped to establish the church on a sound footing. Yet all did not go continually well. Perhaps only a couple of years after Paul wrote the letter to the Ephesians, he wrote a letter to his disciple Timothy, who had been sent to the church. This letter is now known as 1 Timothy. The rich instructions about leadership and conduct within the house of God that we find in 1 Timothy suggest that there were needs and concerns to be addressed among the Ephesians. Timothy superintended the work at Ephesus for some time, and about five years after the writing of Ephesians, Paul wrote his second letter to Timothy, who, by all appearances, remained in a leadership role at Ephesus. Later, the apostle John would make Ephesus his ministry base. Think of the heritage this church held! What an impressive array of spiritual leadership! Paul, Priscilla and Aquilla, Apollos, Timothy and John all ministered there.

It is this rich heritage of spiritual leadership that makes the last mention in Scripture of Ephesus so amazing. Today, we will move forward in time some forty years and see how the church at Ephesus was faring. What had they done with what Paul taught them? Did they continue in the faith? How did God see this church now?

📖 Read Revelation 2:1–7 through carefully and make a list of all the things that were **right** with the Ephesian church.

Worked hard and persevered	Hate the nicolaitans
intolerance of wicked men.	
Test and false apostles and exposed their lies	
Not grown weary under stress and testing	

Four decades after Paul's ministry in Ephesus, there are many things of which one could compliment this church. The people of this church would not tolerate evil men. They *"put to the test"* those who called themselves apostles and even identified those who failed the test (2:2). It would seem they had taken to heart the instruction Paul gave them in his first letter to Timothy concerning standards for those who would lead (see 1 Timothy 3). They were characterized by perseverance and

Put Yourself in Their Shoes
THE NICOLAITANS

The "Nicolaitans" mentioned in Revelation 2:6 were followers of Nicolas (possibly the same Nicolas listed in Acts 6 as one of the "pre-deacons"). This group apparently was a sect which advocated license with regard to sin in matters of Christian conduct, even going so far as promoting sexual promiscuity with the excuse that all sin was forgiven. Tradition holds that to prove his lack of jealousy, Nicolas offered his wife for adulterous affairs.

endurance; they hadn't grown weary of well doing (2:3). Verse 6 compliments them for hating the deeds of the Nicolaitans, apparently a commendable action.

Now, read through Revelation 2:1–7 a second time and make a list of the things that were **wrong** with the Ephesian church.

Forsake their first love

Verse 4 begins with the statement, *"But I have this against you. . . ."* Jesus' message through the apostle John is that the people had "left" their first love. Notice, it does not say they "lost" it, but they "left" it. They had allowed working for Christ to supplant walking with Him.

📖 Looking at Revelation 2:5, what was the prescribed solution to the predicament of the Ephesian church?

Repent and return to their roots.

The problem of leaving their first love was more than just neglect. It was sin. This is seen in the fact that the solution was simply to repent. Revelation gives us a very good explanation of the process of repentance. It begins with remembering—they were to remember from where they had fallen. In other words, they were to "remember what it was like to be close to God." Remembering would lead them to repenting. When speaking of our first love, the passage is not saying that we must feel what we felt as a new Christian. It is not requiring that our faith be lived in a constant state of spiritual infatuation. The idea of staying close to one's "first love" is referring to one's devotion, not emotion. It is saying, "Let Christ be preeminent once again; do not let service take His place."

According to Revelation 2:5, what would the consequences be of not repenting.

lampstand removed ~~And~~ from its place

Word Study

REPENT

The Greek word translated "repent" here (*metanoéō*) literally means "to perceive afterwards" (*metá* [after], implying change, and *noéō* [to perceive]) and has the idea of having "second thoughts," leading to a change in action, usually for the better—in this case, turning to God from sin.

The message from Christ here is emphatic and sobering. If we allow working for the Lord to take the place of walking with Him, there will be consequences. Jesus mentions that He will "remove" their "lampstand." Most scholars see this verse suggesting that Christ will take away the Ephesians' ministry. When you think about it, ministry really isn't what we do for the Lord. It is what He does through us as we walk with Him. That is the message of Jesus' parable of the vine in John 15.

It is worthwhile for us to consider these words to the Ephesian church, for they shed a profitable context for our study in the book of Ephesians. More importantly, they serve as a powerful reminder that starting well does not guarantee finishing well. Sadly, this city, which is situated on the western coast of Turkey, is not known today having for a vibrant church. We should take this anecdote as a warning to our own spiritual lives.

FOR ME TO FOLLOW GOD

No matter how spiritually mature one is, every believer continually faces the ever-present danger of straying from simple, pure devotion to Christ (See 2 Corinthians 11:3). With the letter to the church at Ephesus that we find in Revelation 2, we see the most significant and pervasive danger of all—that of leaving your first love. It is God's great love for us that draws us into a relationship with Him. But, along the way, it is all too easy to get caught up in working for God and lose sight of worshipping God. The solution is not in manufacturing emotions as a new "work," but in coming to grips in a fresh way with God's love for us—*"we love, because He first loved us"* (1 John 4:19).

As we study the book of Ephesians in the days and weeks ahead, we will do well to consider the mistakes they made. We are called in Ephesians 4:1 to *"walk in a manner worthy. . . ."* Clearly, that includes maintaining our first love. As we consider the applications to our personal life from this introductory overview lesson, perhaps the most poignant and practical applications are to be found in that later letter to the church. Let's begin with some personal evaluation. Our "first love," as we said before, is not about emotion, but devotion. It is about the preeminence of Christ in our lives. It is about our personal walk with Him. We can have a relationship **to** God and yet not be developing a relationship **with** God. Intimacy with God is all about spending time with God's Son, Jesus Christ. With that in view, consider the questions below.

 An important thing to consider as we look at the importance of personal devotions is asking the question, "What might keep me from spending time with God?" Consider the possibilities listed below, and check the three that have the greatest potential of getting in the way of consistently spending time with God.

___ Don't know what to do   ___ Lack of a place   ___ Not a priority

___ Changing work schedule   ___ Boredom   ✗ Sin in my life

___ Don't see the importance   ✗ Too busy   ___ Not organized

✗ Not planning ahead   ___ Other _____

Habits are easier to form if we can be consistent. If you can plan to spend time with God the same time every day, it may be easier. But even if you can't, you can still build the habit. It comes down to planning and choice. If you think you don't have time for personal devotions, it may be that you have unrealistic expectations. Maybe you think that if you cannot spend a whole hour in quiet time, then you have failed. Perhaps your goal should be something more realistic. Make it your aim to spend at least five minutes a day with God. What you will discover is that on those days when that is all you can do, you will not be discouraged by feelings of guilt. But you will also find that those five minutes will create a desire for more time with God, and you will make that time as you can.

To make time with God a habit is hard without a plan. You don't want to start each time trying to decide what to do each day. There are many tools that can help you with personal devotions. Let me suggest a few that have been meaningful to me.

- ✓ In months with thirty days, I like to read every thirtieth psalm based on what day of the month it is. For example, if it is the fifth of the month, I read Psalms 5, 35, 65, 95, and 125.

- ✓ Read a chapter of Proverbs. There are thirty-one chapters—this works good with months of thirty-one days.

- ✓ Work through a book of the Bible. Perhaps you can read one to two chapters per day of a particular book.

- ✓ A good devotional book. There are a great many devotional books written to help you spend time with God. My favorite is *My Utmost for His Highest* by Oswald Chambers. It is a classic.

- ✓ Read through the Bible in a year.

The key is not to pick one and feel that is all you can ever do. Vary your time. Be creative in developing your relationship with God. Write prayers to God. Play praise music and sing to the Lord. Go for a walk, praying over your concerns as you go. Keep a spiritual diary, writing your thoughts and struggles. Make sure to allow time for meditation, rather than just piling up information. Whatever I am doing in the Word, I like to read until I sense God speaking to me in a personal way from a verse or verses. Then I will stop there and reread, meditating on what it says. Often that is a springboard to prayer as I talk to God about what the passage is saying to me. Since my main goal is to spend time with God, not just to check personal devotions off my to-do list, I don't worry if I don't finish. I just pick up my reading next time wherever I left off.

I usually begin my time in a brief prayer, asking God to speak to me on that very day. Then I read the Word with whatever plan I am using at the time (I change plans regularly for variety—that works best for me). Journaling helps me to remember what I learn—writing out in a notebook the main thought I saw in the Word, and one or more applications to me personally.

After reading and meditating on the Word, I spend time in prayer, using the ACTS acrostic to guide me (**A**doration, **C**onfession, **T**hanksgiving, **S**upplication). When I get to supplication, I split that time between praying for needs and burdens on my heart, and praying for people that are important to me. As a general rule, if anything is significant enough to worry about, it is important to pray about. As for people, I pray for family, friends, missionaries, unsaved that I know, governmental authorities, spiritual leaders, etc. I've never run out of people to pray for. It may be helpful if you assign a different theme for each day of the week—pray for one or two of those groups each day (e.g., on Sunday pray for spiritual leaders, Monday for coworkers, Tuesday for friends, Wednesday for missionaries, Thursday for the unsaved, Friday for governmental authorities, Saturday for family).

 If the principle of personal devotions is to become a regular habit, you need to have a plan. When you aim at nothing, you are sure to hit it every time. Fill out your plan in the space provided on the next page.

Extra Mile
QUIET TIME

Some "Quiet Time" ideas…

- Read every thirtieth psalm
- Read a chapter of Proverbs
- Work through a book of the Bible
- Buy a devotional book
- Plan to read the Bible in a year

Praying God's Way
PRAYER GUIDELINES

A good guide for time in prayer is the acrostic, ACTS.

A—**Adoration,** worshipping God for who He is—His attributes and character

C—**Confession,** agreeing with God about our sins

T—**Thanksgiving,** worshiping and praising God for what He does

S—**Supplication,** bringing our requests to God

When? When are you going to spend time with the Lord?

_____

_____

_____

_____

What? What are you going to use for a plan? Consider the list above for some ideas.

_____

_____

_____

_____

Where? Where can you have your quiet time that will be free from interruption and distraction?

_____

_____

_____

_____

Who? Whom will you pray for?

_____

_____

_____

_____

"In the morning, O LORD, You will hear my voice; In the morning I will order my prayer to You and eagerly watch."

Psalm 5:3

Taking time to plan is key. But if your time alone with God is to become a habit, you must also have a backup or contingency plan in place for when things go awry. If you miss a day, don't get discouraged. Satan would love for you to give up. We think he wins if we miss a day, but really he wins only if missing a day makes us miss another. If your quiet time starts getting dry, be sure and build in some variety. Change things around. Don't let yourself get stuck in a rut, but at the same time, don't judge the quality of your time with God by emotions. If you have talked to God, if you have learned something from His Word, you should see that as progress.

The most important principle is to make a decision. To not decide is to decide not to do it. Why not make a commitment for the next month to spend time with God every day?

Any deepening love relationship requires spending time together, and a relationship with God is no different. David wrote, *"In the morning I will order my prayer to Thee and eagerly watch"* (Psalm 5:3). Prayerfully consider this commitment to God and formalize it by signing your name.

Close your study with a final word of prayer.

 "Lord, I commit to faithfully spend time with you every day for the next two weeks, and to meet with you with a whole heart. I ask you to speak to me what I need to hear, and to convict me of anything in my heart and life that would hinder my walking with you."

SIGNED _____

Why not take the space provided here, and write out a prayer to the Lord for your own life and what you desire Him to do in the weeks ahead as you study the book of Ephesians.

_____

_____

_____

_____

_____

_____

_____

_____

_____

_____

_____

_____

_____

_____

_____

_____

_____

_____

_____

_____

_____

_____

_____

_____

_____

_____

Notes

Ephesians 1:3-14

"BLESS YOU!"
THE BLESSINGS OF OUR POSITION IN CHRIST

"What has happened to you?" The question is as fresh to me today as it was my freshman year in college when I first became a Christian. With the question, Danny, my best friend from high school, acknowledged that my life had become different. Like many today, I had grown up in a broken home—fractured by my father's alcoholism. My teen years were spent wandering without a father's example and guidance. Instead I followed the crowd into marijuana and drugs. By the time I was a senior in high school, I was not only using them, but also selling them. I was the biggest dealer in school. Spiritually, I was lost. I called myself an atheist, but I was not an honest one. It wasn't that I had studied and wrestled and concluded there could be no God; it was just that I didn't care. I thought the purpose of life was to have as much fun as you could have before you died. Yet with all the adventures and experiences I pursued, fulfillment remained elusive. It still seemed just inches from my grasp. The "highs" I lived for were just mini-vacations from the emptiness I battled. When someone very close to me was arrested and sentenced to prison for selling drugs, it was as if blinders fell off my eyes. I was rudely confronted with the reality that my life was going nowhere. The only difference between him and me was that he got caught.

About this time, the Lord brought a friend into my life that patiently and honestly shared with me what it means to be a Christian. Mack was a fellow I worked with, and at first I wasn't interested in his faith, but as I got to know him, I saw in his life

What has happened to you?

the things I wished were true of mine—peace, joy, love, and contentment. After several months of watching his life, I decided I wanted what he had. With his help, near the end of my first term of college, I asked Christ to come into my life one night at work. It wasn't a huge emotional experience. Charlton Heston didn't come into the room and part the couch we were sitting on. Angel harps didn't begin playing. But I remember a pervading sense of peace and rightness. A few days before, I had been walking across campus to a biology exam and encountered Gideons handing out New Testaments. I took one as a joke, and told the fellow I was walking with that I needed as much help on the test as I could get. That little Bible lay, forgotten, in my backpack until I came home from work that night, a new creation in Christ. I immediately began reading in Matthew's Gospel, and for the first time, the Bible made sense. I encountered Jesus on every page.

I hadn't set about trying to reform my life, but when Danny asked, "What has happened to you?"—I realized my life was changed, different. Within a few short weeks he joined me in the faith. Though he is in heaven now, I have thought a lot about Danny's question. I suppose I am still answering it today. You see, though I knew my life was different, and I knew what I had done, I didn't fully realize all that God did. I am still learning more about all that took place when I first trusted Christ. That which seemed to me a simple choice, set in motion a complex working of God in my life. Maybe you are like me. Do you understand all that changed when you met Christ?

WE HAVE BEEN BLESSED

One of my favorite times of the day is sunrise. It is a beautiful thing to be out in God's creation and to begin with total darkness and to gradually see the growing light until the sun peeps over the horizon. Each morning, God, the master artist, lays out the skies as His canvas and covers it with beautiful colors, welcoming the coming day. For individuals who place their faith in Christ, salvation is as a new day dawning. Our present reality is different than it was before. As we seek to understand more fully this new day that has dawned in our lives, we want to see it as God sees it—from His perspective. That perspective is found nowhere more clearly than in Ephesians chapter 1. We looked at verses 1–3 in the first lesson of this study, but it is necessary that we review those verses briefly now to make sure they are fresh in your mind.

📖 Read Ephesians 1:1–3 and then answer the questions that follow.

How does Paul identify the Christians at Ephesus (verse 1)?

as saints who are faithful in Christ Jesus

_____

_____

What does he wish them (verse 2)?

Grace & Peace from God & Jesus

_____

_____

What does he say they have in Christ (verse 3)?

every spiritual blessing (in the heavenly places)

Did you see what Paul called those Ephesians? He called them **saints!** I used to think the title "saint' was reserved only for people like the disciples or Joan of Arc. But as I studied the Bible, I found that it uses the term to refer to anyone who is a Christian. You may not think of yourself as a saint, but God sees you that way if you have placed your trust in the work of His Son, Jesus Christ! In order for us to be accepted, we have to be "in" the Beloved. That position means that when God looks at us, He sees Jesus. In Ephesians 1:2, Paul wishes the Ephesian "saints" grace and peace. This was a common greeting among Christians back then, and basically he reminds the Ephesian church about what God has given them. Perhaps most impacting in these verses is what he says in verse 3 that they have in Christ. Paul says that they have been blessed with *"every spiritual blessing in the heavenly places in Christ."* In other words, everything that heaven has to offer, we have in Christ.

Some people live their whole lives trying to get things from Christ, yet the truth is that we already have *"all things"* in Christ. When we got Him, we got everything else that there is to get. Theologians call this reality "positional truth"—or things that are true of us because of the position we hold. When a person becomes President of the United States, with that position come the keys to the White House and access to Air Force One. He can stay in a hotel if he wants. He can buy an airline ticket to travel if he so desires. But why would he? His position gives him a free place to live and a free means of travel wherever he needs to go. It comes with the office. Positional truths are those things that "come with the office" of being a Christian. Paul says when we became Christians, God blessed us with every spiritual blessing there is in the heavenly places in Christ. The verses that follow in Ephesians 1 are a partial catalog of these blessings. We'll be looking at this passage verse by verse in our lesson, but we will first set the stage for our study by looking at some verses that speak of what happened when we first met Christ.

📖 Read through 2 Corinthians 5:17. What does it say about the one who is *"in Christ"*?

He's a new creature — the old has passed away

To be *"in Christ"* means we have placed our faith in Jesus and invited Him into our hearts. If we have genuinely done this, then a new day is dawning. We are new "creatures" or a new "creation" as most Bibles translate it. That is a powerful term, since man can manufacture (make something out of something else), but only God can create (make something entirely new). Second Corinthians 5:17 tells us that for such a one, old things have passed away and new things have come. This doesn't mean that new Christians are instantly perfect. For example, other verses make it clear that we need to grow as Christians; however, this verse declares that a new day has dawned. My present experience is different than my past.

"Therefore if any man is in Christ, he is a new creature; the old things passed away; behold, new things have come."

2 Corinthians 5:17

📖 Look up these verses and write down what you learn there about what is different in your life since meeting Christ.

John 1:12

He have THE RIGHT to BECOME children of God.

John 15:15

Jesus counts his disciples as friends instead of slaves, as proven by his trust in them with info. from The Father

Romans 5:1

We are no longer God's enemy when we have faith

Word Study
JUSTIFIED

The word, "justified" means to be declared righteous or just by the penalty for unrighteousness being paid. It refers to our being made righteous in a judicial sense. Our sins have offended Holy God and created a debt which must be paid. We cannot pay that debt ourselves, but through faith in Christ, we can be "justified" by the payment of His death for our sins. An easy way to remember what it means is through this little saying: "justified = just as if I'd never sinned."

These verses share some exciting truths! If I have "received" Christ (welcomed Him into my life), John 1:12 tells me, then I have been given the right to become a child of God. God doesn't take me in as a servant, but as part of His family! John 15:15 reveals that Jesus doesn't consider us slaves, but rather, His friends. Romans 5:1 adds that we have been "justified," and we now have peace with God. Once we were His enemies, but now we are His friends, and even part of the family!

Once we enter into a relationship with Christ, we move into a realm of blessing. It is so important that we understand those blessings though. If we do not know what we have in Christ, we will try to work **for** those blessings instead of **from** them. In Christ, we have already been blessed! God has blessed us with "*every spiritual blessing in the heavenly places in Christ.*"

Ephesians 1:3-14

DAY TWO

BLESSINGS FROM THE FATHER

Several years ago, I was part of a celebration at our local airport. Dozens of Christians gathered there to welcome home a family in our church who was returning from Bulgaria with a three-year-old little girl they were adopting. Excitement was in the air as we saw the plane taxi to the gate. Cheers erupted as the happy parents walked into the terminal with this precious girl, Molly, in their arms. She wasn't sure what to make of us, but warmed up when I said, "Hello" to her in her native tongue. As I led our group in prayer, we thanked God for her and prayed for the new life she would have in this loving Christian family. For her, the whole world had changed. Her first three years of life were spent in an institutional orphanage with dozens of children for each worker to care for. Suddenly she had two adoring parents all to herself. She went from the impoverished country of Bulgaria to the abundance of America. She went from the meager resources of that orphanage to the plentiful provision of this family. We couldn't help but rejoice with her. Yet at three years old, she probably didn't understand right away how her whole life was going to be different. Did you know that you and I have been adopted out of a bankrupt world to live in a new country with our heavenly Father, who has limitless resources? We'll look at that truth today.

📖 Look at Ephesians 1:4–5. What is the spiritual blessing of verse 4, and when did it happen?

> *We chose us (individually or corporately?) to share in His blessing and become Holy and Blameless*
>
> *Before creation*

The blessing here is that God chose (selected) us *"before the foundation of the world"* (meaning "before the foundation of the world was laid" or "before creation"). The creation occurred "in the beginning" of time, but not in the beginning of God. The concept of time as we understand it is not an eternal commodity since it began with the creation and will end after Christ establishes His eternal kingdom. Yet God chose us before time was even invented. It is important to read all of the verse. It says that God chose us *"that we should be holy and blameless before Him."* God's intent is that salvation be much more than simply "fire insurance" (protecting us from the fires of hell). He desires us to be holy and blameless and has guaranteed that we will be that way in heaven since living holy lives is the only way we can have a relationship with Him.

Identify the blessing of Ephesians 1:5 and what you think it means.

> *That adoption as children of God (and therefore heirs in His promises) was set as ~~adopted~~ inherent to salvation from before time*

One of the many blessings we have in Christ is that we have been *"predestined"* to adoption as sons. Through Jesus Christ, we have been adopted into God's family as children. God's predestination accomplishes this blessing. Predestination as a biblical word basically means "to guarantee." In this case, it doesn't refer to salvation but to adoption. In other words, God has guaranteed that all who are saved will be adopted into His family as sons. We are adopted, as verse 5 tells us, *"according to the kind intention of His will."* God could have chosen to save us as slaves instead of as sons. We are His children purely by His grace (verse 6). First John 3:1 celebrates this truth saying, *"See how great a love the Father has bestowed upon us, that we should be called children of God."*

📖 Look at Ephesians 1:6. What does it say about us?

> *God's Grace is freely bestowed upon those in Christ.*

God has freely bestowed grace on us through Christ who is called "the Beloved." The King James Version of the Bible translates the entire statement as *"He hath made us accepted in the Beloved."* I like that word "accepted."

Because God loves His Son, Jesus, He is acceptable to Him. If I am in Christ, then I get to be accepted in Him. Even though I used to be an enemy of God, through Christ I am now His friend. That is my present reality. I am *"accepted in the Beloved."* In Matthew 3, when John baptizes Christ, verse 17 records the words God spoke from heaven. The literal rendering is "This is My son, the Beloved, in whom I am well pleased."

Because we are in Christ, now we are "Beloved sons." We don't have to work for acceptance. We already have that. Our obedience, our service, our faithfulness cannot make us any more accepted or loved than we already are! Trusting God and obeying Him now become responses of gratitude, instead of things we have to do to try and earn a relationship with Him. There is great power in understanding the blessings we have from the Father.

Everything is based upon our being "in Christ." Can we choose to no longer be in christ??

Ephesians 1:3-14
DAY THREE

BLESSINGS FROM THE SON

We've been looking at the many things that are true of us because we are in Christ. In the process, we've found that many of these truths have technical terms in religious and theological circles. They may seem a little intimidating at first, but once we understand what they mean, they become something precious to us. One such term is "atonement." In the Old Testament times, one day a year was observed as *Yom Kippur* ("the day of Atonement"). Every year, sacrifices were made for the sins of the people—to atone for them for a time. Yet each year, the sacrifices had to be made again. But when Jesus came and gave His life for us, His perfect sacrifice atoned for our sins—for all time. Christ's ultimate sacrifice eliminated the need for any more sacrifices.

📖 Read Ephesians 1:7–8.

What blessing do you see here for us?

redemption through His blood.

_____

_____

Practically speaking, what do these blessings mean to you?

With our Redemption fully met already in christ, we are free to live our lives as a celebration of His love instead of wasting it away trying (and failing) to earn it ourselves.

The blessing here is redemption, and means "to release on payment of a ransom." The word draws on the cultural practice of slavery in ancient Jewish life. When people were unable to pay their debts, they were sold into slavery to work them off. They could be redeemed or bought back by a family member or friend who would pay the debt. This is what Christ has done for us. We had a debt we could not pay because of our sins. Because of His love and grace, He paid a debt He did not owe.

Doctrine

ATONEMENT

An easy way to remember what the word "atonement" means is to break it down like this: **atone = "at one."** In other words, atonement, the act of covering over or canceling sin, brings two who are divided back together. Our sins separated us from God, but Jesus' sacrifice "atoned" and made us "at one."

Looking at verses 7–8, answer a few more questions.

What was the payment for our "redemption" (see the first part of verse 7)?

His Blood shed on the cross. Enough of his blood to take His life.

What does this tell you about its cost to Christ?

He paid all that He could pay.

Why do we receive the blessing mentioned in these verses (see the end of verse 7)?

Because God's Grace allows for the substitution of Christ's sacrifice instead of our own. God could have refused the "purchase price" that Christ was willing to pay, but HALLELUJAH! He didn't.

The ransom for us could not have been paid monetarily, since *"the wages of sin is death"* (Romans 6:23). Christ purchased our redemption with His blood, which indicates the giving of life. This was not just any life either, but "God, made flesh," worth far more than any human. The only reason we have received this blessing is the riches of God's grace, which according to verse 8, God has "lavished" upon us. The word "grace" is repeated three times in these first few verses and is showcased as the sole basis for *"every spiritual blessing"* (verse 3) in which God has blessed us.

📖 Take a look at verses 8–10.

What is the blessing mentioned here?

We can know the will of God concerning how salvation is given to man.

God, according to His good pleasure, has revealed to us *"the mystery of His will"*—the summing up of all things, both in heaven and on earth, in Christ. We have been made privy to the plan of God for the ages. Colossians 2:2–3 and Romans 16:25 teach us God's mystery is that He (God) is revealed in a human form (Christ), and thus all wisdom and knowledge are revealed through Him to the world. As 1 Corinthians 1:30 puts it, *"By His doing you are in Christ Jesus, who became to us wisdom from God. . . ."* This mystery is a blessing to us, as 1 Peter 1:10–12 tells us that the mystery of Christ was both the expectation of the prophets and the longing of the angels; yet we have the privilege of both seeing it and experiencing it. What a glorious time in which to live!

When one considers the blessings that are already ours because we are Christians, it seems almost too good to be true. We are *"accepted in the Beloved"* (Ephesians 1:6 NKJV). The One who knows us best loves us most! We have been adopted into God's family and have been redeemed by the payment of His own life. All our sins have been forgiven; grace has been lavished upon

Word Study
GRACE

The word "grace" (*charis*) in the Greek language (the language in which the New Testament was originally written) has the same root word as "gift," and the two words are very similar. The common definition for grace (unmerited favor) is accurate, but the idea is incomplete. God's grace to us is undeserved favor when, in fact, we deserve His wrath.

us; and the mysteries of God's will have been revealed. Truly, we have been blessed with every spiritual blessing heaven has to offer in Christ. And yet, the most amazing thing is, **the best is yet to come!** In 1 Corinthians 2:9, Paul tells us that, *"Eye has not seen and ear has not heard,"* nor has it *"entered the heart of man, all that God has prepared for those who love Him."*

📖 Identify the blessing in Ephesians 1:11–12 and what that means from your perspective.

We have an inheritance from God — Further confirmation of our being made adopted spiritually

The blessing mentioned in these verses is the inheritance of God. There are two equally valid ways of reading this verse. The New American Standard Bible translates it, *"We have obtained an inheritance,"* pointing to us as receiving the blessings of God. An equally legitimate translation could be, "We are made an inheritance," reflecting us as God's inheritance which Christ bought back. It is unclear which is meant here, but both are true, and the concepts seem to be linked in verse 14 (see also Deuteronomy 32:9). We have an inheritance in Christ, but we also are an inheritance which Christ has purchased.

Ephesians 1:3-14
DAY FOUR

BLESSINGS FROM THE SPIRIT

Perhaps the least understood Person in the Trinity is the Holy Spirit. He is often referred to as "it." I can recall as a child singing the Doxology in church: ". . . praise Father, Son, and Holy Ghost," and the last words of that refrain conjuring up images of Casper the friendly ghost with a halo on his head. But the Spirit of God is far from being an impotent cartoon character. He is fully God, and when we become Christians, He takes up permanent residence in our lives (John 14:16–17). Just before the crucifixion, Jesus told the disciples of the Spirit's coming and that the Spirit would minister in their lives. He would be their helper. He would guide them into truth (John 16:12–13). The Spirit would remind them of Christ's words (John 14:25–26) and disclose what is to come (John 16:13). He would also convict of sin (John 16:8–9).

📖 Look at Acts 1:8. What did Jesus say would result from us having the Spirit?

We would receive power to be witnesses

Jesus said we would receive power when the Spirit came upon us. You see, the Christian life is not difficult to live—it is impossible to live in our own power! But when the Spirit of God comes into our lives, He empowers us to do what we could not do on our own. We become witnesses of Him as He works in our lives. We can give testimony that He is real and that He makes a difference in our lives.

When the apostle Paul delivers his list of spiritual blessings in Ephesians 1, he mentions the blessings we have from God the Father, from Jesus the Son, and he doesn't leave out the role of the Holy Spirit either.

📖 Read Ephesians 1:13 and answer the questions below.

What is the blessing mentioned in this verse?

The Spirit comes to seal us, or show ownership of our lives

How do we get this blessing?

By believing what we've heard

The blessing mentioned here is that we have been "sealed" in Him with the Holy Spirit of promise. At salvation, God's Spirit came into our hearts to live as a promise of that which is to come. In order to receive this blessing we had to **a)** listen to the true message, and **b)** believe that message (or place our trust in the Savior that message declared). It is interesting to think about what this verse essentially says. When God's Spirit comes into our hearts, He "seals" us or secures us in Christ. Believers receive the Holy Spirit at the point of salvation. This is the time when the "baptism by the Holy Spirit" occurs (see 1 Corinthians 12:13). Being *"filled with the Spirit"* as Paul speaks of in Ephesians 5:18 is not getting more of the Spirit, but yielding every area of our lives to the Spirit's empowering and direction—having our lives filled with God's Spirit as opposed to self.

📖 Looking at Ephesians 1:14, identify the blessing mentioned in that verse.

That we are "scheduled" or "marked" as God's and awaiting His redemption

The blessing here is that we were given the Holy Spirit as a "pledge" or a down payment. In modern Greece, this same word for "pledge" is used for what we call an engagement ring. It literally means earnest money or a down payment—something given beforehand to confirm what is promised. This same Greek word is used figuratively of the Holy Spirit, which God the Father has given to believers in this present life to assure them of their future inheritance in eternity. It is the promise that God will come for His *"possession,"* the Church, also figuratively called His bride in other Scriptures (Revelation 21:2, 9).

Word Study
SEALED

The Greek word translated "sealed" here speaks of the kind of seal placed on official documents where an imprint was placed in melted wax. Often there were two seals connected by a thread. If the thread was unbroken, it was proof that the document had not been opened and altered since it was written. This same Greek word was used of the Roman seal placed on Jesus' tomb. To break that seal without authorization was punishable by death. It was a mark of guarantee, backed by the full authority of the one who placed it.

FOR ME TO FOLLOW GOD

I hope you are beginning to grasp some sense of how blessed we are to be Christians! To quote an old preacher from the hills of Tennessee, "If that don't light your fire, your wood's wet!" Although all these blessings happened the moment we met Christ, we must grow into understanding them fully. As you can see, most of what we looked at this week came out of the first chapter of Ephesians. Later in that same chapter, Paul writes his prayer for the Ephesian believers: *"I pray that the eyes of your heart may be enlightened, so that you may know what is the hope of His calling, what are the riches of the glory of His inheritance in the saints, and what is the surpassing greatness of His power toward us who believe"* (Ephesians 1:18–19). These truths, as awesome as they are, cannot be grasped at once. God must first enlighten us, so that this information moves from our heads to our hearts. A key step in that enlightening process is taking the time to think through how these truths apply to our lives. At the end of each lesson, we will spend some time in application, helping you to live out the truths you are learning. I hope you will find this helpful.

 As you consider the blessings we have looked at this week, which ones did you already understand, and which ones were new concepts for you?

	Already Understood	New Concept
Accepted in Christ	☑	☐
Adopted into God's Family	☑	☐
Redeemed from Slavery to Sin	☑	☐
Forgiven of All Our Sins	☑	☐
Lavished with Grace	☑	☐
Revealed the Mystery of God's Will	☑	☐
Given an Inheritance	☑	☐
Sealed by the Spirit	☑	☐
Given the Spirit as a Pledge	☑	☐

For those issues that were new to you, it may be helpful to talk with your pastor or a trusted Christian friend to make sure you understand all that is meant by them. If a wealthy relative had died and left you items in his will, understanding what those items were would be a priority. In the same way, understanding all that is already ours in Christ ought to be very important to us.

> *"I pray that the eyes of your heart may be enlightened, so that you may know what is the hope of His calling, what are the riches of the glory of His inheritance in the saints, and what is the surpassing greatness of His power toward us who believe."*
>
> **Ephesians 1:18–19**

Take a look again at Ephesians 1:3. How does the verse instruct us to respond to the blessings God has given us?

By giving him honor and glory

_____

_____

_____

God, who has so richly blessed us, Himself deserves to be blessed (to adore and thank for all benefits) by us. Perhaps the most important place to start in applying this week's lesson is to take some time to thank God for these many blessings. Take a few minutes to go through each of the blessings we looked at as they are listed below, and thank the Lord in prayer for them. You may want to use the space provided as a place to write down this prayer.

Accepted in Christ

_____

_____

Adopted into God's Family

_____

_____

_____

Redeemed from Slavery to Sin

_____

_____

_____

Forgiven of All Our Sins

_____

_____

_____

Lavished with Grace

_____

_____

_____

Revealed the Mystery of God's Will

_____

_____

_____

"Blessed be the God and Father of our Lord Jesus Christ, who has blessed us with every spiritual blessing in the heavenly places in Christ. . . ."

Ephesians 1:3

Given an Inheritance

_____

_____

_____

Sealed by the Spirit

_____

_____

_____

Given the Spirit as a Pledge

_____

_____

_____

 One final application to think about: All that we have studied in this lesson are the blessings that belong to believers. They are of no help to you if you are not a Christian. If you have any reason to question whether or not you really are a Christian, take some time to read through the appendix at the end of this workbook called "How to Follow God." If you aren't sure you are a Christian, then this will help you make sure.

Remember, we are not Christians simply because we go to church or because we read the Bible or because our parents raised us to be Christians. Ephesians 1:13 indicates that to be a Christian we must listen _"to the message of truth"_ and also believe. We will look more fully at what it means to believe in the lesson on faith, but suffice it to say, it is more than simple intellectual belief. It is active trust, and it involves our will.

Notes

Notes

Ephesians 1:15-23

GROWING IN YOUR KNOWING
BECOMING ENLIGHTENED TO THE WAYS OF GOD

In the days before airplanes and high-speed travel, people traveled the world aboard ships. These great passenger liners would often take weeks just to cross the Atlantic. On one such voyage, a ship was enveloped in a great storm. A woman aboard ship left her berth, struggled on deck in the driving rain, and made her way to the helm to ask the captain how serious the situation was. Meaning to encourage her he replied, "Madam, we're in the hands of God." "Oh dear," the lady responded, "I didn't know it was that bad!" How do you feel when the outcome of a situation is totally in the hands of God? Is that knowledge comforting or frightening? Often we fear allowing the outcome of our pursuits to fall in the hands of God. Maybe we are pursuing a job, or a relationship, or maybe just enjoyment of life. So, instead of trusting God, we trust what we do. For employment, maybe we are trusting our grades in school, or making just the right contacts. For a relationship, maybe we trust our performance or our looks. For enjoyment of life, maybe we trust what feels good, even if we know it is outside of God's will.

Are you trusting God in every area of your life? If you are like me, contemplating this question honestly is not a comfortable issue. I see in my own life how easy it is to place my faith in self rather than in God. The Scriptures tell us, "*My righteous one shall live by faith*" (Hebrews 10:38). In other words, we are supposed to trust God. But none of us do that perfectly. We all trust something, but our trust is not always focused in the right direction.

> "The church has surrendered her once lofty concept of God and has substituted for it one so low, so ignoble, as to be utterly unworthy of thinking, worshipping men."
> —A. W. Tozer
> (from *The Knowledge of the Holy*)

The opposite of faith in God is self-sufficiency—faith in self. If you are like me, you find yourself in a state of self far too often. But before you start beating yourself up, let me say that, for most of us, the root problem isn't willful disobedience. It isn't just a matter of us being rebellious. There is a root problem that is to blame for our lack of believing in God. This core problem is an inadequate concept of God, and this disease today profoundly affects the Church. A. W. Tozer, in his book, *The Knowledge of the Holy* wrote, "The church has surrendered her once-lofty concept of God and has substituted for it one so low, so ignoble, as to be utterly unworthy of thinking, worshipping men."

This trend is paralleled by the general biblical illiteracy of American Christians. Some time ago, a Gallup Poll showed that only about half of the Protestant population would turn to the Bible first when the need arose to test their own religious beliefs. Among Roman Catholics that number was only one fourth. Less than half of those who called themselves Christians could name only four or more of the Ten Commandments. Is it any wonder we operate from an inadequate picture of God? How can we know who God is and what He is like apart from what His word reveals?

The point Paul is making in the last half of Ephesians 1 is that our view of God needs to grow. In this powerful prayer for the Ephesian Christians, Paul points to the need for a greater view of God's power, His promises, and a greater view of Himself. In fact, if we look closely, we will find that Paul shows us how this can happen. Let's consider this.

Ephesians 1:15-23

ENLIGHTENED TO GOD'S PERSON (1:15—17)

In 1 John 3:2, the apostle John says, "*. . . when He appears,*" speaking of the second coming of Jesus, "*we will be like Him, because we will see Him just as He is.*" Think about this statement. John is speaking of our "glorification"—the final completion of the process of us becoming like Christ. He tells us that the reason we will "*be like Him*" is because we see Him just as He is. The logical implication of this is that we don't see Him just as He is yet. However high our view of God is, it is inadequate and incomplete thus far. We don't yet see Him just as He is. The more we do, the more we are changed by that vision into His likeness. This seems to be the point Paul is making in this portion of Ephesians. He is praying for enlightenment for the Ephesian believers—that they would see God as He really is.

📖 Paul begins Ephesians 1:15 with the statement, *"For this reason."* Looking back at the context, what do you think is the reason Paul starts this verse this way?

He wants to connect the sealing properties of the Spirit with the faith and love that characterize His people

Specifically, the phrasing Paul uses here indicates a direct link to the verses leading up to verse 15. He has just been speaking of our inheritance. More generally though, the "reason" Paul refers to would seem to include the eight blessings of verses 4–14, which make up our inheritance mentioned in verse 14 and the *"every spiritual blessing"* mentioned in verse 3.

📖 Read through Ephesians 1:15–16.

For what traits does Paul recognize the Ephesians?

Faith and Love

Why do you think he picks these two out?

they constitute the two greatest commandments AND are the required foundation for christ-like behavior

Why do you think Paul includes thanksgiving in his prayer?

To show his value assigned to Faith and Love

Extra Mile

FAITH, HOPE, AND LOVE

The apostle Paul wrote about half of the New Testament. The books he wrote are called epistles (the cultural term for letters) because they were letters he wrote to individuals and churches. In almost every letter he wrote, he emphasized three attributes: faith, hope, and love. Take some time to read the following passages where these three attributes are mentioned.

- **1 Corinthians 13:13**
- **Colossians 1:4–5**
- **1 Thessalonians 1:3**
- **1 Thessalonians 5:8**
- **2 Thessalonians 1:3–5**
- **1 Timothy 1:1–5**
- **1 Timothy 1:14–16**
- **2 Timothy 1:12–13**
- **Titus 2:2, 13**

Almost as an aside, Paul mentions to the Ephesians that he has heard of their faith (or trust) in Christ, and the love they have for each other. It is important to notice that these positive traits seem to be related to what Paul prays about when he unceasingly gives thanks for them. This "thankful" praying is set up against the supplication or request that follows. Paul first thanks God for what they have, and then makes request for what they need.

One might not catch the significance of faith and love in more than a general way simply by reading Ephesians, but they are part of a trio of spiritual attributes Paul discusses at length. Paul says in 1 Corinthians 13:13 that three things will "abide" or last: faith, hope, and love. You see this same trio repeated in almost every one of his epistles. Faith and love are found here in verse 15, and hope is seen in verse 18. These three traits are significant in that, to a degree, they gauge the level of our spiritual maturity. The Ephesians are commended for their faith and love, and Paul prayed for them in the area of their hope.

Paul's inclusion of thanksgiving indicates that there was reason for encouragement at their spiritual state and that God was responsible for where they were. It is ironic however, that after being commended for their love for the saints, some thirty years later, they are condemned for "leaving their first love"—their love for the Lord (Revelation 2:4).

📖 Now, read through verses 15–17 as a unit.

For what exactly does Paul pray?

That the Ephesians will complement their external strengths (faith & love) with renewed internal ones (wisdom & revelation)

How does the phrase, "Father of glory" relate to Paul's request?

Paul is specifically praying that God would reveal Himself in the fullest sense to the Ephesians. The rest of the chapter delineates as to the dimensions of such knowledge. By calling our Lord *"the Father of glory"* Paul seems to be emphasizing His worth and value. It seems as if the Ephesians were in need of a higher view of God. That doesn't necessarily reflect negatively on them, for no matter how high our view of God is, it isn't high enough.

In verse 17, Paul prays that they will have a *"spirit of wisdom and of revelation in the knowledge of Him."*

What is the difference between the spirit of wisdom and the spirit of revelation?

What do you expect will result when they have them?

Word Study
SPIRIT

The phrase "*a spirit of wisdom*" in Ephesians 1:17 is mistranslated "*the spirit of wisdom*" in the King James Version. The word "spirit" in the Greek (*pneúma*) is "anartherous," meaning it has no definite article (no word "the"). The Greek word for spirit literally means "breath." What Paul is praying for is a "breath of wisdom." Just as God breathed life into the first man, He must breathe wisdom into us. This idea goes hand in hand with the word "revelation."

The term in the Greek language for revelation is *apokálupsis* (from which our English word "apocalypse" is derived) and literally means "to uncover or unveil." Paul is praying that they would know God fully. The word "revelation" indicates that this will only happen as God "unveils" Himself, which would necessitate praying. God is knowable because He makes Himself known. God is too great for many to reach Him or understand Him on their own. We need revelation. The word for "knowledge" here is *epígnōsis* (from *epí* [upon], and *gnōsis* [knowledge]), meaning "knowledge upon knowledge." *Epígnōsis* refers to full, experiential knowledge. In this case, it refers not to knowing about God, but to knowing Him intimately.

Think of where Paul has taken these believers thus far. He began by spending the first fourteen verses of this book showing them who they are, and now he moves toward helping them understand who God is. Tomorrow we will see Paul expand on this theme. Paul is telling them what they need to believe before he tells them anything else. Later on, he will move into instructing the Ephesians in what they need to do about these beliefs, but belief always comes before behavior. Right thinking leads to right living.

ENLIGHTENED TO GOD'S PROMISES (1:18)

Ephesians 1:15-23
DAY TWO

Have you ever stubbed your toe on something because you tried to make your way through a darkened room without turning on the light? I have made that mistake too many times to count. I have often thought that the main reason God gave us the little toe was for finding furniture in the dark, and mine is especially good at it. There is a simple solution to this dilemma. It is called a light switch. Walking is much easier (and safer) in a lighted room than in the dark. The same is true in our spiritual lives. Walking with God is easier when we walk in the light. To walk with God is made more difficult when we stay in the dark. Paul wants the Ephesian believers (and us) to have light so they can know how to "*walk in a manner worthy*" (Ephesians 4:1). Today we want to examine further Paul's prayer for "enlightenment."

📖 Read over Ephesians 1:18 carefully.

What do you think the phrase, "*the eyes of your heart*" means?

_____

_____

_____

_____

What does it mean that the eyes of our hearts "*may be enlightened*"?

_____

_____

_____

_____

_____

The "heart" in modern cultural use refers to the inner man, the very center and core of life. The King James Version translates the word "heart" here as "*understanding.*" Paul's prayer in essence is that the Ephesians would not just possess "head knowledge." Head knowledge is that which **we possess;** heart knowledge is that which **possesses us.** Paul is asking that the "*light of the world*" (John 8:12) would shine in our darkened hearts (see Romans 1:21; Ephesians 4:18).

Did You Know?

? THE EYES OF YOUR HEART

The phrase "the eyes of your heart" in Ephesians 1:18 is a figure of speech. Obviously, our physical hearts do not have eyes, nor is the blood-pumping muscle being referred to here. Western thought uses the term "heart" metaphorically to refer to the inner man. Though the Greek manuscripts used to translate the New American Standard Bible and other translations use the word "*kardia*" (heart) in this verse, other manuscripts use the word *diánoia. Diánoia* means "through the mind," relating to one's "understanding" (as it is translated in the King James Version).

📖 Read Ephesians 1:18–19 together now. What is the expected result of this enlightenment for which Paul prays—the three things he wants the recipients of this letter to know?

_____

_____

_____

_____

_____

Paul wants believers in Ephesus to have the eyes of their hearts enlightened "so that" they can know certain things. He mentions three specifics here. First, he prays that they would know what *"the hope of His calling"* is. Second, he desires that they would know the wealth of *"the glory of His inheritance in the saints."* Another way of saying this might be "His glorious inheritance in the saints." Third, Paul prays that they would understand the *"surpassing greatness of His power toward us who believe."* We'll be looking at that third area tomorrow.

What do you think is meant by the *"hope of His calling"*?

_____

_____

_____

_____

The "hope" spoken of here (which 4:4 identifies as a singular hope [*"one hope"*]) does not refer to wishful thinking (e.g., "I hope it is sunny tomorrow") but rather, the desire of some blessing with the expectation of obtaining it. This type of hope carries the idea of confidence and security. Our hope is in our calling. Our hope as believers is our eternal fellowship with God in heaven. The book of Titus uses the word "hope" three times, and each instance is linked to eternal life. Titus 1:2 speaks of the hope of eternal life as being promised by God *"who cannot lie."* Titus 2:13 refers to us looking for *"the blessed hope,"* which is identified as the coming of our Lord for us. Titus 3:7 says that we are *"heirs according to the hope of eternal life."* Clearly hope is an important thing.

Compare Ephesians 1:18 with Ephesians 2:12 and write what you learn.

_____

_____

_____

_____

_____

In Ephesians 2:12, Paul tells us that before knowing Christ, the Ephesians were without hope and without God—the two go hand in hand. Believers have a hope, and we need to be enlightened as to what that is, for it will affect how we live. What would the opposite of hope be here? The opposite of hope would be hopelessness or despair. Paul tells us in 1 Corinthians 15:32 that if the dead are not raised and there is no afterlife, then the most logical philosophy is, *"let us eat and drink, for tomorrow we die."* This explains why many unbelievers live as they do and view believers as they do. As he says in 1 Corinthians 15:19, *"If we have hoped in Christ in this life only, we are of all men most to be pitied."*

Unbelievers live as they do because they have no hope of anything more than this life. If we don't understand our future hope, we may live that way too. Hope doesn't help if we are uninformed of it.

What do you think verse 18 means by the phrase *"the riches of the glory of His inheritance in the saints"*?

_____

_____

_____

_____

Certainly we are rich because we are God's, but in a tangible way, God considers Himself rich because we are His. As it says in Deuteronomy 32:9, *". . . the Lord's portion is His people . . . His inheritance."* A work of art derives its value from two sources: a) the person who creates it, and b) the price someone is willing to pay for it. Our creator is the Almighty God who also purchased our redemption for the incomparable price of His Son.

The apostle Paul wants us to know what our future holds. He recognizes that a right understanding of our future has great practical effect on how we live in the present.

ENLIGHTENED TO GOD'S POWER (1:19–20)

The city of Oak Ridge, Tennessee didn't exist in the 1930s. It was created at the beginning of World War II to house a scientific community working on a top secret project with military applications. I know about it because I grew up near there and my mother and stepfather both worked there. This community was built almost overnight in the middle of nowhere to keep the project as secret as possible. We now know that this project they were working on was the first atomic bomb. As World War II came to an end in Europe in 1945 with the defeat of Germany, it continued in the Pacific. Though it became apparent that Japan was not going to win the war, it was also apparent they would not surrender. Faced with a lengthy ground invasion that would cost countless American soldiers their lives, President Truman opted instead to make use of this new weapon developed in Oak Ridge. The first atomic bomb was dropped on Hiroshima, Japan, and the nuclear age began. The devastation was incomprehensible. The world had never known such awesome military power. As a huge mushroom cloud rose up, an entire city was leveled, and millions of

Word Study
GLORY

Why does Paul use the word "glory" in verse 18? Actually, the word "glory" appears five times in this first chapter (1:6, 12, 14, 17, and 18), and in every instance it is directed toward God, who is most deserving of this description. God is glorified through the riches of His inheritance. It is not arrogant of God to expect glory since, in all the universe, He alone is worthy of glory.

Ephesians 1:15-23
DAY THREE

> *"And what is the surpassing greatness of His power toward us who believe. These are in accordance with the working of the strength of His might."*
>
> Ephesians 1:19

lives lost with that one blast. Until it had been deployed, only a handful of people had any concept at all of the power of such a weapon. But once its power was demonstrated at Hiroshima and again at Nagasaki, the Japanese military quickly capitulated. The war was over.

The years that followed World War II have seen the proliferation of nuclear weapons and the creation of bombs thousands of times as powerful as those dropped on Hiroshima and Nagasaki. While none of us would debate the overwhelming and awe-inspiring destructive power of a nuclear weapon, it is nothing compared to the power of God. While an atomic bomb has the ability to inflict mass destruction, God alone has the power to create and recreate. The heavens and the earth came into being by the word of His mouth. When men nailed Jesus to the cross, and laid Him in the tomb, God had the power to raise Him from the dead. One of the requests that Paul prays for the Ephesian believers is that they would be enlightened to God's great power, the greatest power the world will ever know.

Look at Ephesians 1:19. What do you think it means that God's power toward us "surpasses greatness"?

_____

_____

_____

_____

The Greek word used here for "surpassing" is *huperbállō*, from *huper* (over), and *bállō* (to throw). It literally means "to throw over" greatness. In other words, *huperbállō* takes the concept of greatness and throws it into a whole different realm. This great power of God that surpasses anything else it could be compared to is directed toward us.

Compare Ephesians 1:19 with 2 Corinthians 4:7 and write what you see.

_____

_____

_____

_____

_____

_____

Did You Know?
EARTHEN VESSELS

When Paul says in 2 Corinthians 4:7 that the majestic message of Christ is placed in *"earthen vessels"* of human beings, he is painting a vivid, cultural picture. The earthen vessel of Paul's day was the most common, ordinary, container available. It was neither fancy nor expensive. A good modern parallel would be a washed out, plastic whipped cream tub or a jelly jar.

Paul, in 2 Corinthians 4:7, makes the point that God has created mankind in such a way that when He chooses to work through us, it will be obvious that the power is in God and not us. He makes mankind an *"earthen vessel"* so as to showcase the *"surpassing greatness"* of His power. This may be what Paul has in mind in Ephesians 3:21 when He speaks of God receiving eternal glory *"in the church."*

How according to these verses was this power of God proven?

_____

_____

_____

_____

The most complete and visible demonstration of God's power in history, as Paul mentions here, was the resurrection of Christ. This was a feat which only the Author of life could accomplish. Mankind can take life, but only God can give it.

Think about what Paul is saying here. There is no power shortage with God. Verse 19 actually contains three different Greek words for power. The first word (translated "power") is *dúnamis,* from which we get our English words "dynamite" and "dynamo." This word emphasizes God's ability or capability. The second word (translated "working") is *enérgeia,* from which we get our English word "energy." In verse 19, *enérgeia* emphasizes the active exhibition of God's power. The third word (translated "strength of His might") is *krátos* and has more of the idea of the presence and significance of God's force or strength than the exercise of God's strength. What is the point? God has more than enough power. If God can raise Jesus from the dead, doesn't He have enough power to handle whatever comes your way?

ENLIGHTENED TO GOD'S PURPOSE (1:21–23)

Paul's phrase, *"that the eyes of your heart might be enlightened"* paints an interesting portrait when viewed in the context of the specific things he wants the Ephesians to see. It is almost as if he is showing them the treasure rooms of a great castle. As the tour guide, he takes us room by room and shines a lantern in each place, showing us yet another space filled with inexpressible riches. He has taken us to the throne room and shown us the wealth of God Himself. He has taken us to the bank vaults and shown us the wealth of His promises. Paul has taken us to the mechanical room and revealed God's great power. But the tour is not over yet. He has still more to show us.

📖 Read through Ephesians 1:19–20 again. What did God do after He raised Jesus from the dead?

_____

_____

_____

_____

_____

After God raised Jesus from the dead, He seated Him *"at His right hand in the heavenly places."* The term *"right hand"* points to a position both of honor and of authority. For example, at a dinner party, the most honored guest would sit at the "right hand" of the host. But that is not the only context of this terminology. He who was allowed to sit at the "right hand" of the king (in the chair to the right of his throne) would operate with his authority. This is where the colloquial expression "right-hand man" comes from.

What is the point of Ephesians 1:21?

_____

_____

_____

_____

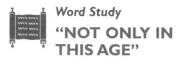

Christ has been given the most prominent position in all of creation for both this age and the one to come. This is only appropriate since, as Paul points out in Colossians 1:16, *". . . by Him all things were created, both in the heavens and on earth, visible and invisible, whether thrones or dominions or rulers or authorities—all things have been created by Him and for Him."*

What do verses 22 and 23 relate about the purpose of God?

_____

_____

_____

_____

_____

_____

It has been the purpose of God from eternity past to place Christ as supreme head over all. The remarkable part in all of this is that He has been given as *"head over all things to the church . . . which is the fullness of Him."* Through God's grace, we the Church, get to share in the position of Christ because positionally we are *"in Christ."* This phrase *"in Christ"* or its equivalent appears 27 times in Ephesians, with most of these appearances coming in the first three chapters of the book.

Compare verses 20–23 with Genesis 1:26–31 and write what you learn.

_____

_____

_____

_____

_____

_____

Genesis 1:26–31 makes it clear that from the beginning it has been God's intent to have mankind reflect His image. Through sin, that image of God was marred and perverted and could no longer be clearly seen. What God is accomplishing through Christ is "re-creating man in His image," and restoring him to his original position of reigning over creation.

Think of what Paul has instructed us in this section of Ephesians. He has revealed our need to know God more fully. He has reviewed God's promises of our future hope and inheritance. He has reminded us of God's awesome power. And he has related to us God's eternal purpose for Christ—to place Him over the entire created realm. These are things we need to know.

Word Study
"NOT ONLY IN THIS AGE"

The King James Version translates this phrase in verse 21 as *"not only in this world"*; however, the Greek word translated "world" in the King James Version is not the normal word for the planet (*kosmos*) but is the word *aion*, from which we get our English word "eon." *Aion* has the idea of an indefinitely long period or lapse of time. The word "age" doesn't necessarily refer to a specific length of time, but rather, to a period of God's dealings. It may point specifically to the Millennium, or, more generally, to eternity.

Did You Know?
KING OF KINGS

Ephesians 1:21 tells us God has placed Jesus *"far above all rule and authority and power and dominion."* In traditional Jewish thought, there was believed to be a hierarchy of angels, and the terms, *"rule and authority and power and dominion"* were the titles given to them. It is unclear if they are listed in order of authority or what that order is.

FOR ME TO FOLLOW GOD

What is the "abundant life"? What is the best thing in life, bringing more joy, delight and contentment than anything else? It is none other than knowing God. *"Thus says the Lord, 'Let not a wise man boast of wisdom, and let not the mighty man boast of his might, let not a rich man boast of his riches; but let him who boasts boast of this, that he understands and knows Me. . . .' "* (Jeremiah 9:23–24a). What is "eternal life"? John 17:3 says, *"And this is eternal life that they may know Thee, the only true God, and Jesus Christ whom Thou hast sent."* What were we made for? To know God. To what aim should we set ourselves in life? To know God. (This paragraph is adapted from *Knowing God* by J. I. Packer, InterVarsity Press [1993], p. 29.)

We have looked at many different principles about knowing God. What is the most important one? It is this: what you do when you spend time with God is not nearly so important as <u>that</u> you spend time with God. Spiritual growth is not the result of a dramatic experience, but a lot of small steps. You cannot be changed by one experience into spiritual maturity any more than you can become a full-grown adult by eating one meal. You will eat many meals in your lifetime, and probably they won't all be identical. Each will satisfy in its own way, but you will hunger again. Think of spending time with God as one meal in the whole plan of your spiritual nutrition. If you are doing something that isn't satisfying your spiritual hunger, then change your diet. But whatever you do—don't give up eating. The following questions are meant to help you keep "growing in your knowing."

 The only way to get to know God is to spend time with Him. On average, how many days a week do you really spend quality time talking with God? (Circle a number on the line below.)

$$\longleftrightarrow \quad 0 \quad 1 \quad 2 \quad 3 \quad 4 \quad 5 \quad 6 \quad 7 \quad \longrightarrow$$

When you spend time with God, what is the average amount of time spent (in minutes)?

_____

_____

How would you rate the quality of your times with God?

_____

_____

_____

What criteria do you use to determine the success of your times with God?

_____

_____

_____

_____

What do you need to do differently to improve your times with God?

_____

_____

_____

_____

_____

One of the requests that Paul prayed on behalf of the Ephesian believers is that they would be enlightened to know what is the "*hope*" of their calling. Knowing what our future is has great affect on the present. In fact, 1 John 3:3 tells us, "*everyone who has this hope fixed on Him purifies himself, just as He is pure.*" Knowing we will one day see Jesus face to face gives us the moral courage to live pleasing to Him today.

APPLY How aware are you of your hope in Christ?

_____

_____

_____

What present attitudes could be improved by meditating on your hope in Christ?

_____

_____

_____

_____

Paul also prays that we would be enlightened to "*the surpassing greatness of His power toward us who believe*" (Ephesians 1:19). Not only does God have the power we need; He has more. His power surpasses greatness.

APPLY In what areas of your Christian walk do you feel the need for more power?

_____

_____

_____

_____

_____

In what areas of your Christian walk do you feel the need for more power?

Perhaps the most important application to our study this week is a simple observation from verses 16 and 18. All that Paul has said in this passage is in the context of a prayer. We will not know these things that Paul speaks of simply through study. Study we should, but we also need revelation—we need God to reveal them to our hearts, not just our heads.

As you close out this week's lesson, why not write out a prayer for God to reveal these things to your heart…

Jonathan — Renewed Energy
Randy — Dillgence, Worry
Chris — To Resist Satan
Clay — Prioritize Relationship
Adam — Purity of Motives
Mark — Effective Prayer, Worry

Notes

Ephesians 2:1-10

FROM GRAVEYARD TO GLORY
GOD'S TRANSFORMATION OF OUR LIVES

Winston Churchill was without a doubt one of the greatest and most influential figures of the twentieth century. But he was an unlikely candidate to become a hero. In fact, for several years, most politicians in Great Britain viewed him as the last remnant of the Victorian age—hopelessly out of touch with modern times. Just prior to World War II, his political star that had once shined bright was now fading as his intransigence and years of speaking his mind had made him enemies on all sides. After World War I, most thought Churchill's career was on the decline. He was viewed as a warmonger in an age of pacifism. But when Neville Chamberlain's strategy of appeasement to the German dictator, Adolf Hitler, proved a dismal flop, suddenly Churchill's political star rose from the proverbial ash heap.

Winston Churchill was sixty-five years old when he first became Prime Minister—an age where most men think of retirement, not saving the free world. He became the only man who could unite all political sides as well as the nation to stand against Nazism. When he became Prime Minister of Great Britain, the whole of Europe was enveloped in the Nazi expansion of World War II. Virtually every nation on the continent had either been conquered by Germany or had joined in alliance with the maniacal Hitler. By the end of 1940, England stood alone against the military might of the fascists. The British people were hopelessly outnumbered, and some perhaps thought the wisest course would be to sign some sort of peace treaty with Hitler.

No "comeback story" is as impressive as the eternal shift that happens when a penitent sinner places his trust in Christ.

But the indomitable Winston Churchill wouldn't think of it. He defied Hitler to conquer the British Isles, and his statement to the House of Commons, "I have nothing to offer but blood, toil, tears, and sweat," became the backbone of British resistance. Eventually, the United States joined Britain as allies and helped win the war, but, for many months, Great Britain stood alone amidst a sea of war with Winston Churchill at the helm.

When one ponders the path of Winston Churchill's career, there is no doubt that his political resurrection was nothing short of impressive. It is a remarkable thing for one to achieve his greatest human glory after everyone considers him finished. But God used Churchill's rebound to be instrumental in a resurrection of another sort—one of biblical proportions—for Churchill was one of the proponents of a Jewish homeland in Palestine. Public sympathy for the Jews was at its height after World War II as news of the atrocities of the Holocaust began to be realized. The Promised Land was British territory at the time, and in 1948 it was largely the work of Great Britain that brought the nation of Israel back into existence. Against all odds of history, a nation that did not exist for some two thousand years was reborn.

Nonetheless, the new life of Churchill's politics and even the new life of the nation of Israel are not as great as the eternal shift that happens when a penitent sinner places his trust in Christ. When a pagan becomes a saint, there is nothing to compare with it, for it is a resurrection in truth and reality, not in hyperbole. It is as dramatic a change as a dead body coming to life and being placed on the throne. Such a person has gone from graveyard to glory.

Ephesians 2:1–10

SIN'S WORK AGAINST US (2:1–3)

I have often wished I had a testimony of growing up in a Christian home, meeting the Lord early, and never having wandered. As I shared in Lesson 2, that was not my experience. I grew up in a broken home with an alcoholic father. My high school years were spent in rebellious, illegal, and destructive behaviors. Taking drugs and selling drugs were the center of my life—running from one high to the next. You might say I put the "high" in high school. I was a professing atheist when I started college. I believed human beings to be the meaningless byproduct of a meaningless universe. If there was any advantage at all to such a background, perhaps it is that I can still vividly remember and fully appreciate what it was like to be an unbeliever. I can still call to mind the nagging emptiness of my heart, the lack of purpose and direction in my life, and the seeming meaninglessness of my existence. I know what it is like to be lost. If you came to Christ at a young age or have always been taught about the Lord, that distinction may not be as clear in your mind. You may know in theory that you were lost without Christ, but you may not have a frame of reference that illustrates the difference salvation makes. You may only understand it by trusting what God says about the unbeliever.

When the apostle Paul wrote to the believers at Ephesus, he wrote to people who could appreciate the change Christ had made in their lives. They were mostly Gentiles who came to Christ as adults. Yet even they needed to be reminded of the changes that had taken place in their lives spiritually and what they were like before.

📖 Take a look at Ephesians 2:1.

Why does Paul call us "dead" even though we're alive?

Because without the hope of Christ to overcome the power
of sin, there is no relief from a cancer inside us —

What do you think is meant by "trespasses and sins"?

Choosing to inhabit spaces called off-limits by God
actions borne of self-reliance and rebellion

Although we are all alive physically, until Christ enters our lives, we are spiritually dead. This is why Christ points in John 3 to our need not just for physical birth, but for spiritual birth as well. In Genesis 2:17, God warned Adam that the penalty for disobeying His only command would be death. After Adam and Eve violated that command, they didn't immediately die physically (though the aging process had already begun), but they did die spiritually. This is what Paul points to in Romans 6:23 when he says, "*. . . the wages of sin is death.*" This "spiritual death" means we are dead in our ability to relate with God, since those who worship God must do so in spirit (John 4:24).

In Ephesians 2:1, the apostle Paul uses two different but related terms to describe our fallen state. "*Trespasses*" is from the Greek word *parapíptō*, meaning to stray or to fall alongside the prescribed path. "*Sins*" comes from the word *hamartía*. This term originally carried the idea of missing the mark as with hunting or military use—to miss the target you are aiming for. Applied to us, sin means we miss the mark or fall short of God's standard of holiness and righteousness. These two terms do not point to different kinds of sin, but the whole of sin. It is this point Paul is making in Romans 3:23 when he says, "*. . . all have sinned and fall short of the glory of God.*"

We are "dead" in our trespasses and sins. If all we were was spiritually sick, then all we would need from God would be a little help—reviving and resuscitation, and then we could take it from there. But being dead, our only hope is resurrection. We are completely in need of God, and only He can raise the dead.

📖 Reflect on Ephesians 2:2 and answer the questions that follow.

What do you think is meant that we walked according to "*the course of this world*"?

We did what we thought was right in our own eyes and in our
own counsel. Problem is — our vision is so short-sighted
and our wisdom is so incomplete that we repeatedly failed to
hit the mark.

THE PROMPTERS OF SIN:

- the fallen world system in which we live
- the fallen nature of the flesh
- the fallen angel (the devil) who fights God's ways

Who is the "prince" and "spirit" spoken of here?

Satan

When Paul speaks of us formerly walking according to *"the course of this world,"* he implies that we used to walk in step with the world system around us—the accepted lifestyle of the day. Not only did we walk in step with the world, but also with the devil. Both the words *"prince"* and *"spirit"* here are obvious references to Satan. In 2 Corinthians 4:4 (NIV), Satan is designated the *"god of this age,"* and in John 12:31 (NIV), he is called the "prince of this world."

📖 Now contemplate Ephesians 2:3.

According to verse 3, what is an additional promoter of our sin?

our nature

Why are man's actions sinful?

His motives are based in self

In verse 2, we saw the role of the world and the devil in our sin. Here we see a third component—our lustful desires and mind (literally "thoughts"). We see these same three identified throughout Scripture—the world, the flesh, and the devil. They prompt man toward sin—deviating from God's plan of righteousness. Man's actions are sinful because his desires and thoughts are sinful and his nature is corrupted. Sin doesn't begin in the actions but in the desires. This is why Jesus equated the thoughts of murder and adultery with the actions in the Sermon on the Mount (see Matthew 5:21–28).

What do you think the phrase *"children of wrath"* means?

we, in many respects, are the product of the sin before us.

The phrase *"children of wrath"* comes from a characteristic Hebrew expression that is difficult to translate into English, let alone interpret. The term may suggest that wrath is an integral part of our sinful nature, or as Charles Ryrie suggests in the *Ryrie Study Bible,* that we are children deserving of wrath. Both interpretations have merit. If Paul has the former in view, then he is probably highlighting our need to lay the old way of living aside. If the latter is in view, then it highlights the grace of God in removing the guilt and punishment for our many sins.

What a wretched state we were in before we met Christ! It is important for us to understand who we were so that we can understand more fully who we are and what changes salvation has wrought in us.

God's Work for Us (2:4—7)

Where would man be if left to his own devices? Certainly, man is able to make a mess of things, but is man able to clean up that mess? Is he capable of rescuing himself from the quicksand of his own choices? The answer to that question is the single most defining issue of Christianity and every other religion. In fact, it is within the answer of that question that we find the fundamental difference between Christianity and every other religion the world has ever invented. The common denominator of every major world religion is the idea that man could (and should) save himself from the pit of his own mistakes. Confucius basically says, *If you had listened to me, you would have avoided the pit.* The New Age movement says, *You really aren't in a pit; you only think you are because you don't realize you are God.* Hinduism says, *If at first you don't succeed, try, try again* (in this life and the ones after it). Modern secular psychology says, *It isn't your fault; blame the guy that sold you the shovel.* Judaism says, *If you keep these 642 rules and that doesn't get you out of the pit, fall back on the fact that Abraham is your father.* Humanism says, "Future generations will learn from your mistakes and evolve beyond them" (if they study hard enough). Islam says, *Prayer and sacrifice will get you out of your pit.* . . . and so on, and so on, and so on. Every religion has its own slant, but they all end up at the same place—*You made the mess, and you have to get yourself out of it.* All of them, that is, except Christianity. The message of Christ is radically different from every other religion. The Christian faith asks only this—admitting you cannot get out of your pit and asking God to do what you cannot do.

When Christianity takes root in our lives, it faces the reality of who we are in ourselves, but offers who we can be in Him. While we were still dead, Christ died for us. The Christian message acknowledges that we are dead in our sins, disobedient to our Maker, and destined for winds of wrath, and then says, **"But God. . . ."** Every other religion says man must try as hard as he can to reach God. The formula for these "isms" may be a little different. One says be moral, while another says meditate, and still another says educate. But in the end, they are all about what **man** can do. The message of the Cross is not what man can do to reach God, but what **God has done** to reach man.

Ephesians 2:4 begins with the word "but." What is the significance of this contrasting term? The transitional word "but" in this case signals the major shift in thought of the entire passage of 2:1–10. It ushers in a classic "before and after" scenario, and contrasts our former unregenerate state with our new position in Christ. We were dead, disobedient, and destined for wrath—**but God intervened.**

📖 Look at Ephesians 2:4.

What does it mean that God is *"rich in mercy"*?

He has so much that he can simply give it away freely to all who ask.

> *Religion has been defined as "man's attempts to reach God through his own efforts." Christianity is "God's attempts to reach man through Jesus Christ."*

> "But God, being rich in mercy, because of His great love with which He loved us, even when we were dead in our transgressions, made us alive together with Christ (by grace you have been saved)...."
>
> Ephesians 2:4

Why does God's mercy relate to *"His great love"*?

It is the mercy that allows God to express His great love for us.

In a very tangible sense, mercy is the logical outworking of God's great love when it is directed toward His children. The Greek word for mercy is *éleos* and has the idea of tender compassion toward the needs of others. Because God loves (*agapē*) us, He is rich in mercy toward us.

📖 Read through Ephesians 2:5.

What do you think the statement *"even when we were dead in our transgressions"* means?

He didn't require us to "get it all right" before he applied mercy and love. He did it while we still couldn't even acknowledge Him.

How does this relate to us being saved by grace?

By definition, it was NONE of our doing.

Since God's mercy was manifested while we were still "dead" in our sins, it is impossible for us to have aided in the process of salvation through our efforts. Paul connects this mercy to the obvious necessity of salvation being by grace.

What do you think it means that God *"made us alive together with Christ"*?

Spiritually, we are as alive now as Christ is.

This wording may be a reference to the resurrection of Christ. However, some ancient manuscripts do not say *"made us alive together **with** Christ"* but rather, read *"made us alive together **in** Christ."* In this case, it would not be a direct reference to the resurrection of Christ, but rather to our spiritual births. In either case, our spiritual births seem to be the main emphasis. Since being "dead" refers to being spiritually dead, then being "made alive" would logically mean becoming spiritually alive. It is Christ's resurrection that makes our new lives possible.

The phrase, "in Christ," or its equivalent appears twenty-seven times in the book of Ephesians. More often than not, it is referring to what we call **position-**

al truth—things that are true of us because of the position we hold. As we learned in lesson two, positional truths are those things that "come with the office" of being a Christian. To be "in Christ" means we have placed our faith in Jesus and invited Him into our hearts. If we have genuinely done this, then a new day is dawning. As 2 Corinthians 5:17 states, we are new "creatures" or a new "creation" (as most Bibles translate it).

📖 Now take a look at Ephesians 2:6 and answer the questions that follow.

What do you think is the significance of our being raised up with Christ?

we are given all of the blessings, authority, power —
essentially ACCESS To GOD through our being with Christ
spiritually

_____

_____

_____

_____

_____

What is the point of us being *"seated . . . with Him in the heavenly places"*?

You and I are *"in Christ,"* that is, when He was raised and ascended, so also were we. This is the essence of what we call "positional truth." Because we are "in Him," His position becomes our position as well. It is this co-resurrection with Christ that makes it possible for us to *"walk in newness of life"* as Paul points out in Romans 6:4. Because positionally we have been *"seated . . . with Him in the heavenly places"* as a result of being *"in Christ Jesus,"* we are able to appropriate and experience the benefits of this high position. First, the position provides a secure place in heaven for eternity (Matthew 28:20). Secondly, it means that we will reign with Him for eternity (Exodus 15:18). Thirdly, as 1:20 points out, we are seated with Him at the *"right hand of God"*—the place of honor.

Doctrine

YOU MAY BE SEATED!

The apostle Paul tells us that Jesus is "seated" in the heavenly places. Ephesians 1:20 tells us that He is seated at the right hand of the Father. The emphasis of His being seated speaks of the fact that His work is finished, completed. Since we are seated with Him, it speaks as well of our work being finished (inasmuch as it relates to salvation).

MORE OF GOD'S WORK FOR US (2:8–9)

Ephesians 2:1-10

DAY THREE

The Bible tells us that *". . . all have sinned and fall short of the glory of God"* (Romans 3:23). That means everyone has sinned—from Billy Graham to Hugh Hefner and all points in between. Each of us has sinned, because each of us are sinners. Here in Ephesians, Paul tells us that before we met Christ, we were dead, disobedient, and deserving of wrath. If you stopped there, it would be a pretty depressing message. But Paul does not stop there. After he has taken us as low as we can go, he says, *"But God."* When we could do nothing to help ourselves, God did what was needed. He has made us alive in Christ; He has saved us; He has resurrected us; and He has seated us in the place of highest honor. What we could never do, He has done in Christ. Sin's work against us is no match for God's work in us! Paul is not finished telling us all of God's work for us. Today, we want to continue looking at all God has done for us.

📖 Read through Ephesians 2:7 and answer the questions below.

Ephesians 2:4–6 speaks of some of the many things God has done for us. What according to verse 7 is God's reason for these workings?

_____

_____

_____

_____

What do you think the phrase *"ages to come"* means?

_____

_____

_____

Why do you think it is plural?

_____

_____

_____

God *"made us alive,"* *"raised us up,"* and *"seated us with Him in the heavenly places"* so that He might establish the church as an eternal display of *"the surpassing riches of His grace."* As chapter 1 shows, God's workings toward us are by His grace and for His glory. He is glorified when ages to come see all that He has done for His children. According to *Vine's Greek Dictionary,* the meaning of the word "ages" isn't so much referring to the actual length of time but rather a period marked by spiritual characteristics. Being plural, it likely points to the period of peace on earth that will transpire after Christ's second coming and may also refer to Christ's eternal kingdom.

📖 Look at Ephesians 2:8.

Paul emphasizes again in this verse (see also verse 5) that we are "saved by grace." What do you think this term means?

_____

_____

_____

_____

How would the verse's meaning be changed if the phrase said "saved by faith"?

_____

_____

_____

_____

_____

To be "saved by grace" is very different than to be "saved by faith." To be saved by grace means that our salvation is entirely *"a gift of God; not as a result of works."* In fact, the word "grace" in the Greek has the idea of a gift though a different word is used for the word gift here. If we are saved **by** faith instead of **through** faith, then faith becomes a work in and of itself. Certainly faith is essential to the salvation process, but it is not the principal agent. Apart from grace, we could not be saved regardless of how much faith we have.

📖 Read through verse 8 again.

What do you see as the significance of the words *"saved through faith"*?

_____

_____

_____

_____

Why can't we be saved through our own power?

_____

_____

_____

_____

What is the point of salvation being *"a gift of God"*?

_____

_____

_____

_____

Although we are saved only because God has poured out His grace upon us, faith is needed to appropriate God's grace. As Hebrews 4:2–3a points out:

> *. . . we have had good news preached to us, just as they also; but the word they heard did not profit them, because it was not united by faith in those who heard. For we who have believed enter that rest. . . .*

It is not salvation "by grace **plus** faith," but salvation "by grace **through** faith." Consider a paycheck as an illustration. We experience the benefits of the check because we endorse it, but that is not the reason we are paid. Faith is like our endorsement of God's gift of salvation. It doesn't earn us salvation, but it is necessary for us to access the benefits of it. These verses seem to imply that salvation requires both God's work (grace) and man's work (faith), but it should be noted that man has a choice to make only because of the choice God has already made in showing His grace. Apart from God's grace, faith is impotent. This seems to be reiterated by the statements *"not of yourselves"* and *"a gift of God."* Faith is necessary, but God wants our trust not to be in our faith, but in His grace.

When we consider that we have been saved by grace through faith, the logical question arises, "What exactly have we been 'saved' from?" We saw at the beginning of this chapter that before Christ we were "dead" in our tres-

Word Study
GIVING

There are two verbs which could be translated "to give": the common *didōmi* (to give), which has a variety of meanings according to the context, and *doreomai* (to grant), with the inherent emphasis on the gratuity of giving, showing the generosity of the giver. It is this second root word which is used here in Ephesians 2:8.

passes and sins. Romans 6:23 tells us that "*the wages of sin is death*." Paul seems to have that in view here when he speaks of their state before meeting Christ, and it is from this "death" that we have been saved. It is important to understand that the western concept of being dead (cessation of existence) is biblically inaccurate. Man is eternal in one state or another, and since biblical death refers to separation, we are "saved" from eternal separation from God.

📖 Take a look at Ephesians 2:9.

How would salvation as a result of works lead to boasting?

_____

_____

_____

_____

Why is it important that "no one should boast"?

_____

_____

_____

_____

God alone is worthy of glory, and He has arranged our salvation so that He gets glory from it. Salvation by works would enable us to boast, as it would be related to our accomplishments. But salvation by grace gives all the glory to God where it rightly belongs.

Ephesians 2:1-10
DAY FOUR

GOD'S WORK IN AND THROUGH US (2:10)

Sin's work against us made us dead. God's work for us has made us alive again. He has raised us to new life. He has saved us by His grace, not by our works. He has done it in such a way that we cannot boast. But if you stopped there, you might get the idea that salvation is all of God with nothing for man to do. While we are not saved **BY** works, we are saved **FOR** works. God wants good works to be part of our lives. He wants to do through us things that will give Him more glory. He wants to manifest Himself to others through our lives. He wants to do a work in us so He can do a work through us.

📖 Read over Ephesians 2:10 reflectively. Why is it significant that we are *"His workmanship"*?

_____

_____

_____

_____

God created all living things—including us. We have no room for boasting because all that we are and do is possible only because of Him. When we do good works, it is only because that is what we were created to do. There is no such thing as a self-made Christian.

Read verse 10 again. Why is it important to know that we were "*created in Christ Jesus for good works*"?

_____

_____

_____

_____

_____

Understanding that we were created for good works keeps us from looking at our salvation merely as "fire insurance" to protect us from the fires of hell. God wants our Christian lives to be adorned with good works. He has given each believer a spiritual gift to enable us to do good works. He doesn't want us to live our Christian lives as spectators.

What do you think it means that our good works are "*prepared beforehand that we should walk in them*"?

_____

_____

_____

_____

This statement contains an important and often misunderstood point about service. God wants good works to be part of our lives. But this does not mean that we are simply to "work for Jesus" in the same exact ways. God has specific works in which He wants us involved. To walk in the works He has for us, we must walk in fellowship with Him, following His lead and call. Think about that message. God has special things prepared that He desires to do only through us—not through anyone else. There is a plan for each life that bestows incredible significance on each of us. Our works may not be flashy or even noticed, but if we do what God has for us to do, they will make an eternal difference.

We often quote verses 8 and 9 without verse 10. How does verse 10 balance the truth in the other verses?

_____

_____

_____

_____

Although we are saved "by grace through faith" and not as a result of works, that doesn't mean that works aren't a part of the Christian life or aren't important. In fact, according to verse 10, it was for good works that we were created, and it is God's will that we "walk" in good works. This verse also states that we were "*created in Christ Jesus for good works*." Before we took our position in Christ, true good works were not possible.

> *"For we are His workmanship, created in Christ Jesus for good works, which God prepared beforehand so that we would walk in them."*
>
> *Ephesians 2:10*

FOR ME TO FOLLOW GOD

In John 10:10, Jesus said, *"I came that they might have life, and might have it abundantly."* In other words, Christ came that our lives might be full and meaningful. The sad truth, however, is that most Christians aren't experiencing that abundant life. Billy Graham estimates that ninety to ninety-five percent of all believers don't experience the kind of life Christ promised. The office of the U.S. presidency is a powerful position, yet the title would be of no use to its holder if the commander in chief didn't make use of the power that position provides. In the same way, our position in Christ makes limitless power available to us; yet that power won't affect our day-to-day experience if we are uninformed about it or don't choose to make use of it. God "delivered us from the domain of darkness" (see Colossians 1:13), yet so many believers still stay there. The time has come to get out of the graveyard and make use of our tremendous position in Christ.

 If you have never placed your trust in Christ, then sin is working against you. The most important application for you is to ask Christ into your life. If you are already a Christian, are you enjoying the liberty you have in Christ, or are you still bound by the habits of the old life in the graveyard of sin? Use this graph for an honest evaluation of your present Christian life:

Graveyard ◄——— 1 ——— 2 ——— 3 ——— 4 ——— 5 ——— 6 ———► Glory

Have you come to grips in your own life with the reality that you are saved by grace?

It is important to realize that we are saved by grace—but that is the beginning, not the end. Colossians 2:6 exhorts us, *"as you have received Christ Jesus the Lord, so walk in Him."* In other words, we live the Christian life every day the same way we started it—"by grace, through faith." Godliness is not the result of trying harder, but of trusting God more. If we could make ourselves righteous by trying hard, we wouldn't need a savior.

📖 Take a look at Galatians 2:21 and summarize its message as it relates to your salvation and sanctification.

_____

_____

_____

_____

_____

Here, in Galatians, the apostle Paul equates trying to be justified by the works of the law with "nullifying" the grace of God. To nullify means to make of no consequence or impact. God wants our Christian walk to be the result of trusting Him moment by moment as we walk in fellowship with Him. When we try to justify ourselves by our own striving instead, we rob ourselves of the empowering work of His grace. In essence, we are saying, "I don't need the cross of Christ." This idea seems to be the point of Paul's statement in Ephesians 2:10 that we are *"His workmanship."*

If we could make ourselves righteous by trying hard, we wouldn't need a savior.

How much does knowing that you are His workmanship affect the way you live?

_____

_____

_____

_____

Once we understand what it means to be His workmanship instead of our own, then we are well on our way to walking in the good works He has prepared for us. It is an awesome and exciting thought to recognize that God has a plan for our lives. He has prepared beforehand, good works—acts of blessing that He wants to accomplish through no one but us. Walking in those works begins with identifying and acknowledging how God has uniquely gifted us. If you have never studied the subject of spiritual gifts, you might want to check out the study on spiritual gifts in the **Following God Discipleship Series.**

Once we know what our spiritual giftedness is, then we need to look at what our passions are—what are those things that motivate us personally in the area of ministry. Maybe you have a passion for youth, or for teaching the Word, or for showing compassion. Your passions are one of the ways God guides you in where you put your giftedness to work. Another way He guides is through opportunities—open doors He places before us. Consider these three and see if you can identify a pattern of God's leading.

My giftedness seems to be _____
I am passionate about the following types of ministry:

_____

_____

_____

_____

The opportunities or open doors I see at present are…

_____

_____

_____

APPLY Remember, if God has prepared good works for us beforehand and He wants us to walk in them, you can be confident He will show you what those works are. The question we should ask ourselves is, *Are we looking to Him as we look for opportunities?* A good rule of thumb for knowing if a place of service is God's will is this:

DESIRE + OPPORTUNITY + NO RED FLAGS = GOD'S WILL

If we have desires but no opportunities, our desires probably aren't God's will (at least not yet). He is big enough to open any doors needed. If we have opportunities but no desire, either the opportunities aren't His will or our hearts aren't right. In either case, we need to continue seeking Him before acting on it. If we have the desire and the opportunity, we can move forward and trust that if it isn't God's will, He will place some "red flags" of warning

Do you know where to serve?

to show us we are heading the wrong way. God wants us to know His will even more than we do. If our heart is surrendered, we can trust our desires and His leading. He'll let us know if we head the wrong direction.

Why not close out this week's lesson by writing out a prayer to the Lord in the space below, asking Him to show you the good works He has prepared for you.

_____

_____

_____

_____

_____

_____

_____

_____

_____

_____

_____

_____

_____

_____

_____

_____

_____

_____

_____

_____

_____

_____

_____

_____

_____

_____

_____

_____

_____

_____

Notes

Notes

Ephesians 2:11-22

SHALOM! PEACE!

THE DIVINE WORK OF RECONCILIATION

World War I was supposed to be the war to end all wars. The rest of the twentieth century proves that hope unfounded. Yet, even at the time, a thorough view of history should have made it obvious how impossible a hope that was. I have heard it said that in over three thousand years of recorded history, the world has recorded less than three hundred years of peace. If the term peace is being defined as no war anywhere on the planet, three hundred years is probably too high a figure. During that time, it would seem the only lasting peace to be found in the region of earth has been on the moon. The "Sea of Tranquility" there enjoys peace, but perhaps only because there are no humans there. On the twenty-seventh of November, 1895, Alfred Bernard Nobel established with his estate, the Nobel Peace Prize. He had amassed a huge fortune from his patent for dynamite and the manufacture of explosives and perhaps felt some measure of guilt or responsibility for the military uses of his inventions. It was his desire to promote peace. Yet the Nobel Peace Prize was not able to prevent the two world wars and scores of smaller military actions around the globe in the last century, nor does it seem likely that it will prove any more effective in the current one. I don't mean to make light of the Nobel Prize—peace is such a worthy goal that it certainly is worth the effort. Yet experience makes us skeptical.

It was at Christmastime in 1863 that Henry Wadsworth Longfellow penned the words to the now famous carol, "I Heard the Bells on Christmas Day." At that moment—the height of the Civil War—his son was languishing in a hospital with wounds suffered at the battle of Gettysburg. Scores of

The "Sea of Tranquility," a huge crater on the moon, has known uninterrupted peace for centuries—but that is only because there are no humans there.

America's youth who had fought on that bloody ground already lay beneath it. The war would eventually result in over six hundred thousand casualties—more American lives lost than in all her other wars combined. As the bells rang out on that Christmas morning of 1863, peace was nowhere in sight. "Hate is strong," wrote Longfellow, "and mocks the song of 'Peace on Earth, Good Will to Men.'" The entire nation felt the weight of this brutish conflict, but none more than the men who fought it, and the families of those wounded and killed in it. Yet, as Longfellow heard the Christmas bells ringing, another message came to his anguished heart. As he heard the bells ring long and deep, he thought, "God is not dead, nor doth He sleep. The wrong will fail, and right prevail with 'Peace on Earth, Good Will to Men.'" He had grasped a realization that each of us must come to eventually. If ever there is to be peace, it will not be the work of men, but God. This is the crux of the apostle Paul's message here in Ephesians chapter 2.

Ephesians 2:11-22

DAY ONE

THE DIVIDING WALL (2:11—12)

The center of spiritual life for the Jew in Palestine was always the Temple. It was the divinely-appointed place for the people of God to worship Him. Several times a year, devout Jews would make their way to Jerusalem to observe the holy feasts and festivals of their faith. Gentiles—all those outside the "chosen people"—were invited to worship Jehovah, but they could not enjoy the full privileges of the natural-born Jew. The Temple grounds were divided by a great barrier called the "Dividing Wall" beyond which a Gentile was not allowed to go. Above the entry way of that wall, a plaque warned of the penalty of death for any Gentiles attempting to gain entrance. This was a fact of which Paul would come to have some first-hand knowledge. In Acts 21:27–40 we have the record of false accusations made against Paul that he brought Greeks into the Temple and had *defiled this holy place.* The crowds were in a turmoil, and Paul would have been beaten to death were it not for the timely intervention of Roman soldiers. Man could not reconcile Jew and Gentile—the division was too great. But what man could never do, God did. As we will see today, the work of the cross brought true reconciliation to men and broke down the barrier walls.

📖 Verse 11 begins with the word "therefore." Reflect on the verses that come before and identify what you think this "therefore" points to.

_____

_____

_____

_____

_____

The transitional word "therefore" invites us to look backward—back to the peace Christ offers between God and man made possible by grace and accessed through faith. As we look forward, we see that peace between men—specifically here between Jew and Gentile—will only be realized on the ground of grace. As peace between God and man is realized through the cross, peace between men is now possible.

60 FOLLOWING GOD – THE BOOK OF EPHESIANS

What do you think it mean that the Gentiles are "Uncircumcision"?

_____

_____

_____

The Greek word for Gentile is *éthnos* (from which our English word "ethnic" is derived) and usually points to the heathen as distinguished from the Jews or believers. The Gentiles were called "uncircumcision" (see Romans 2:25) because they didn't have this outward evidence of inner spirituality. Even as Christianity began to take hold, the subject of circumcision was often still a "hot button" issue though God did not intend it to be this way.

Why do you think Paul considers it significant that circumcision is performed "*in the flesh by human hands*"?

_____

_____

_____

_____

Paul emphasizes here that circumcision is performed "*in the flesh by human hands*" so that the reader will recognize circumcision for what it is—an imperfect, outward sign of an inner-spiritual reality. The New Testament parallel over which many stumble is baptism. The physical act of baptism doesn't save you; it is merely the outward expression of the inner heart toward God.

📖 Reflect on Ephesians 2:12. What "time" do you think Paul is referring to here?

_____

_____

It would appear that Paul is referring to the "time" of Ephesians 2:1–3—that period before those church members at Ephesus become Christians. The notion that Paul is referring to a prior era is evidenced with the use of the word "formerly" in verse 11. Probably most of them became Christians around the same time, since Paul founded the church only a few years earlier. This reminder Paul gives of their past shows the distinction between their spiritual experience and those who had grown up in the Jewish faith.

Looking at verse 12, make a list of all the things the Gentiles were without?

_____

_____

_____

_____

_____

Here Paul presents a list of five things the Gentiles lacked before they responded to the message of the gospel. First, they were without Christ.

Did You Know?

CIRCUMCISION

Circumcision was originally given as an outward sign of the Abrahamic covenant (see Genesis 17). In Jeremiah 4 and 9, God draws a link between the physical state of circumcision (causing sensitivity to the male reproductive organ) and spiritual circumcision (possessing a heart sensitized toward God). The Jews had lost the symbolic, inner meaning behind the practice.

Second, they were excluded (or "alienated") from the nation and people of Israel. Third, they were strangers to God's covenants of promise to Israel. They had not entered into those promised blessings of God. Fourth, they were without hope. They lacked anything to place their hope in. Finally, and most significantly, they were without God.

Paul tells the Ephesians twice in Ephesians 2:11–12 to "remember" these things. Why?

_____

_____

_____

_____

The admonition to the Ephesians to "remember" their former state, it would seem, is designed to move them toward an appropriate response of gratitude. Verses 8–9 make it clear that one cannot work his way to God, but as verse 10 points out, that doesn't mean we don't do good works. It was for them that we were created. Paul is helping the Ephesians identify what they should be grateful for, and in chapters 4–6 he shows them appropriate ways to express that gratitude.

Ephesians 2:11-22

DAY TWO

"I have had many friends . . . and few difficulties. I have gone from wife to wife and from house to house, visited great countries of the world, but I am fed up with inventing devices to fill twenty-four hours of the day."

—the suicide note of cartoonist, Ralph Barton

THE DIVINE WORK (2:13–14)

How old were you when you met Christ? I didn't become a Christian until I was in college, and I have regrets for the wasted time and worthless deeds I took part in before I met Christ. I must confess, sometimes I look with some measure of envy at those who came to Christ early in life and never wandered from the faith. I wish I hadn't made so many mistakes and missed so many years of walking with the Lord. Yet, if there is any benefit to coming to Christ later in life I suppose it is this: I can remember clearly what it was like not to know the Lord. I vividly recall the nagging emptiness, the lack of meaning and purpose, the futility of my life. The cartoonist, Ralph Barton captured with brutal eloquence the despair of life without Christ in a note he left on his pillow before taking his life: "I have had many friends, great successes, and few difficulties. I have gone from wife to wife and from house to house, visited great countries of the world, but I am fed up with inventing devices to fill twenty-four hours of the day." Though I never despaired to the point of suicide, I can relate with the haunting emptiness we hear in Ralph's words. The divine work of the Cross means that empty lives can be filled—joy can put within our hearts the satisfaction that fleeting periods of happiness cannot. I think part of Paul's goal here for the Ephesians is to remind them of all that they were saved from. I hope I never forget that.

📖 Take a look at Ephesians 2:13.

From what exactly were the Ephesians *"formerly . . . far off"*?

_____

_____

_____

To what have they now "been brought near" through Christ?

_____

_____

_____

How were they "brought near"?

_____

_____

_____

The Gentiles were formerly far off from all the focuses of hope for Israel—their identity as God's chosen people, the promise of Messiah, the covenants, the hope of heaven, and God. Now, through Christ, they were able to share in the "blessed hope" Paul speaks of in Titus 2:13—eternity with Christ. The means of this wondrous work was the blood of Christ. His sacrificial death satisfied the demands of righteousness, paying for our sins so that both God's love and His holiness could be expressed.

Look at the following verses and summarize what you learn about the significance of the "blood of Christ."

Hebrews 9:22

_____

_____

_____

_____

Ephesians 1:7

_____

_____

_____

_____

Acts 20:28

_____

_____

_____

_____

Romans 5:9

_____

_____

_____

_____

"And according to the Law, one may almost say, all things are cleansed with blood, and without shedding of blood there is no forgiveness."

Hebrews 9:22

1 Corinthians 11:25

_____

_____

_____

_____

Hebrews 10:29

_____

_____

_____

_____

Hebrews 10:19

_____

_____

_____

_____

In Hebrews 9:22, we see that *"without the shedding of blood there is no for-giveness."* Christ didn't die to be an example of sacrificial love; He died to purchase our forgiveness. In Ephesians 1:7, we were taught that the shedding of Christ's blood accomplished redemption and forgiveness. Acts 20:28 instructs us that the shedding of Christ's blood purchased the Church. Romans 5:9 teaches the shedding of Christ's blood justified us and saved us from God's wrath. In 1 Corinthians 11:25, we learn that the shedding of Christ's blood established a new covenant. Hebrews 10:29 says that the shedding of Christ's blood sanctified us (made us holy). Finally, in Hebrews 10:19, we see that the shedding of Christ's blood opened up God's presence to us. So much was done, yet we can never forget the price that was paid!

📖 Read Ephesians 2:14 and then reflect on this question: Why do we need peace?

_____

_____

_____

_____

_____

_____

_____

It is important to understand and to be reminded that not only has sin alienated us from God (see Isaiah 59:2), but it also alienates us from each other (Galatians 5:19–20 says *"the deeds of the flesh . . . are . . . enmities, strife, jealousy, outbursts of anger, disputes, dissentions, factions. . . ."*). As this passage in Ephesians points out, it is Christ who brings peace—peace between God and man, and peace between each other. Needless to say, this peace is the peace of Christ.

RECONCILED BY THE CROSS (2:15—18)

Christians value morality and rightly so. The moral principles of the Law of God teach us what holiness is. Yet, in our lifting up of morality, we run the danger of communicating the message that the central aim of religion is morality. In fact, it is not. God gave us the moral law not to be an end in itself, but as a tutor to lead us to Christ. If we could be moral on our own, we wouldn't need a Savior. We could not keep God's law. Our breaking of God's laws placed us in bondage to sin. Through the work of the cross, Christ abolished the hold of judgment the Law had on us. He did not do away with the Law. That would have sent the message that righteousness didn't matter. Instead, He abolished the Law by fulfilling it. Today we want to continue looking at the reconciling work of the Cross and not just on its effect on our relationship with God. We also want to consider its impact on our relationship with man.

📖 How, according to verse 15, did Christ bring peace between Jews and Gentiles?

_____

_____

_____

_____

_____

Christ brought peace between Jews and Gentiles by dealing with the "enmity," the law of the commandments. In this case, the reference is probably not to the "law" in a general sense, but rather, to the specific "ordinance" of the dividing wall. Christ, by making righteousness available to the Gentiles as well as the Jews, has opened up for all who are in Him the very presence of God (Hebrews 10:19). The word used for "made," referring to Jews and Gentiles being one body, is literally "create."

What do you think it means that Christ "abolished" the Law?

_____

_____

_____

_____

_____

The Greek word for abolished, *katargeō* (from *katá* [down] and *argeō* [inactive]), literally means "to reduce to inactivity." Christ didn't destroy the Law; He rendered it inoperative to us. Verse 16 indicates that Christ *"put to death"* the law. It is important to recognize that contrary to contemporary Western thought, death is not "cessation" (or ceasing to exist); it is "separation." Christ separated us from the Law. In Matthew 5:17 Jesus said, *"Do not think that I came to abolish the Law or the Prophets; I did not come to abolish but to fulfill."* The Word for "abolish" in Matthew 5:17 (*katalúō*) is different than what is found in Ephesians 2:15 and has the idea of setting aside. Christ came to make the Law inactive on us, but not to set it aside as unimportant.

Did You Know?
THE DIVIDING WALL

The Jewish Temple was separated into two halves—the outer half (the court of the Gentiles) and the inner half (the court of the Jews). Archaeologists have discovered a plaque that hung on the Dividing Wall, and the inscription warned Gentiles of the death penalty for entering the court of the Jews (see also Acts 21:27–36). Jesus did away with this barrier and made both groups into one body in Him.

How did Christ bring peace between God and man (verse 17)?

_____

_____

_____

Christ reconciled both Jews and Gentiles to God through His substitutionary death on the cross. Romans 6:23 tells us that *"the wages of sin is death."* Christ paid that debt for us. As it says prophetically in Isaiah 53:5–6, *"He was pierced through for our transgressions, He was crushed for our iniquities; . . . the Lord has caused the iniquity of us all to fall on Him."*

 Take a look at Ephesians 2:17. Why is it that "peace" has to be preached?

_____

_____

_____

_____

Apart from proclaiming peace, there is no way for those in rebellion to know, understand, and act on the terms of that peace. Years after World War II there were Japanese soldiers discovered on several islands still waging war who had never heard of the peace established in 1945 when the Emperor surrendered. Likewise, there are many who are uninformed of the possibility of peace with God.

Verse 17 is a quotation of Isaiah 57:19. Read the verse in its original context and write down any observations.

_____

_____

_____

_____

This quotation from Isaiah appears in the context of God's just and divine right for judgment, yet His gracious choice to show mercy. Peace is only possible because God, at the expense of sacrificing His son, makes it possible. To appropriate this peace, according to Isaiah 57:15, requires a contrite and lowly spirit. Conversely, 57:21 tells us that *"there is no peace . . . for the wicked."*

 In light of the context, what do you think is the significance of verse 18?

_____

_____

_____

_____

Verse 18 tells us that *"through Him"* (in His name and by His working) we both (Jew and Gentile) have our access or admission into the presence of God. Salvation by grace establishes a common ground between Jew and Gentile who approach the Father through the same Spirit (the Holy Spirit). Since both are now on equal footing before God, there is no longer room for boasting by the Jew.

"But He was pierced through for our transgressions, He was crushed for our iniquities; the chastening for our well-being fell upon Him, and by His scourging we are healed. All of us like sheep have gone astray, each of us has turned to his own way; But the LORD has caused the iniquity of us all To fall on Him."

Isaiah 53:5–6

FELLOW CITIZENS (2:19—22)

Recently, I saw a group of immigrants on a news show who had completed all the requirements for citizenship and were being "sworn in." You could see the emotion in their eyes. I couldn't help but feel their joy as they waved tiny American flags and cheered at the end. I had the sense that it was the fulfillment of a dream. For nearly three centuries, people from all over the world have come to America to find freedom and opportunity. The arms of "Lady Liberty" still beckon. People can come as visitors, but there is a permanent commitment in those who become citizens. There are rights and privileges that accompany this commitment. We should be able to relate to this scene. You and I have had a swearing in ceremony of our own. As Paul spoke in Philippians 3:20–21, *"Our citizenship is in heaven, from which also we eagerly wait for a Savior, the Lord Jesus Christ; who will transform the body of our humble state into conformity with the body of His glory. . . ."* Through Christ's work on the cross, for the first time in history, it became possible for Gentiles to have full rights of citizenship in the Kingdom of God.

Compare verse 19 with verse 12 and write down what you observe about how the two verses contrast.

_____

_____

_____

_____

_____

Before receiving Christ, the Ephesians were strangers (this alludes to the statement in verse 12, *"strangers to the covenants of promise"*) and aliens (although a different Greek word, the word "excluded" in verse 12 could be translated "alienated." Apparently, the title "aliens" points to the Ephesians' former state of being *"excluded from the commonwealth of Israel,"* but now they are *"fellow citizens"* with Israel.

Compare verse 20 with verse 12 and write down the things you learn.

_____

_____

_____

_____

_____

Before receiving Christ, the Gentile Ephesians were *"separate from Christ."* Now Christ had become the Cornerstone (preeminent part) of their foundation—that upon which they build their lives. One should not take this verse to mean that Christ is only the Cornerstone, since elsewhere He is identified as the Foundation (see 1 Corinthians 3:11), the Door (see John 10:7), the Temple (see John 2:19), and the Builder (see Matthew 16:18). He *"fills all in all"* (see Ephesians 1:23).

> **"Our citizenship is in heaven, from which also we eagerly wait for a Savior, the Lord Jesus Christ; who will transform the body of our humble state into conformity with the body of His glory..."**
>
> **Philippians 3:20–21a**

Compare verse 21 with verse 12 and write down your observations.

_____

_____

_____

_____

_____

Word Study
CORNERSTONE

In the days before bricks and blocks and blueprints, construction was even more challenging than it is today. A good finish to a sturdy and safe building required a good beginning. Special attention was paid to the placing of the first stone, called the cornerstone, to be sure it was square and level and positioned properly. It served as the frame of reference for everything else that would be added. Jesus is the cornerstone of our faith.

Before receiving Christ, the Ephesians were alienated from God and man (specifically the people of God—the Jews) and were thus without hope. Now they are being *"fitted together"* with the future promise of total unity as God's temple which is explained in the next verse. This would certainly be great cause for hope and joyful expectation. First Peter 2:4–8 identifies that every believer is a *"living stone"* in God's architectural effort, with the end product being a heavenly temple in which He will dwell.

Compare and contrast verse 22 with verse 12 and write down what changed in Christ.

_____

_____

_____

_____

Before receiving Christ, Paul's audience was *"without God."* Now they were in the process of being prepared as His dwelling place. This idea points to the three-part promise of the Old Testament—"I will be your God, you will be my people, and I will dwell in your midst."

Truly, everything changes when Christ comes into a life. In Ephesians 1, Paul emphasized the new realities of our position in Christ. Here in chapter two, he has given these added emphasis by contrasting them with what we were like before. Every believer must make certain not to forget the change Jesus has wrought.

Ephesians 2:11-22
DAY FIVE

FOR ME TO FOLLOW GOD

Peace with God is an awesome thing on which to reflect. The truth that we have been reconciled to our Creator through the Cross ought to cause our hearts to overflow. As a result of this peace with God, it now becomes possible for us to be at peace with each other. So why is this worthy dream not always reality? Because there are still so many who have never heard the message of peace, let alone responded to it. St. Augustine said "Lord make me an instrument of Thy peace." What a tremendous privilege it is that we who have received God's peace have been given the opportunity to be messengers of that peace. This is truly "Good News" that man can have peace with God. All the world looks and longs for peace, yet there can be no peace on Earth until men have peace with God. As important and significant as this is, it is sad that this area is rarely the priority it should be, Jesus Christ died to make reconciliation possible. You and I must live to make the message of reconciliation personal. Through Christ we all have access to God the Father. We must tell this "Good News" to all who will listen! *Blessed are the peacemakers, for they shall be called sons of God* (Matthew 5:9).

 As you reflect on this week's lesson, you must realize that information alone won't make us godly. It is only as that information is moved into application that change occurs. Reflect on these questions and seek the application the Lord has for you personally in this week's lesson.

Do you take seriously your responsibility to communicate the truth of Christ to others (be honest)?

_____

_____

_____

_____

Which of the following are you willing to do to improve in this area?

___Meditate on 2 Corinthians 5:14–21 ___Pursue training

___Be accountable to someone ___Take a step in faith

___Pray for an opportunity ___Pray about your attitude

___Pair up with someone experienced

 Take a few minutes to reflect on your friends, coworkers, and family—those who make up your personal world. Let me challenge you to come up with a "top ten" list—the ten people you would most like to see come to know the Lord.

_____

_____

_____

_____

_____

_____

_____

_____

_____

Once you have made your list, why not copy it down and slip it into your Bible as a regular reminder to pray for these people. It is not our persuasion but our prayer and trust in the persuasive work of God in their hearts that will make people open to Him.

"WHOEVER WILL CALL UPON THE NAME OF THE LORD WILL BE SAVED" (Romans 10:13). That is how one starts life as a Christian; that is how one lives life as a Christian.

Why not make a "top ten" list of those in your life you would most like to see come to Christ and tuck it into your Bible as a reminder to pray.

Has God brought someone in particular to mind of whom He wants you to share the message of Christ?

_____ (name)

Most of our application this week has focused on the need others have for the peace of the Lord. But that is not the only need. Look to your own heart. Christ Himself is our peace, yet we often look for it in other places. To what do you generally turn to find peace?

Why not close out this week's lesson by expressing your heart to the Lord in a written prayer?

_____
_____
_____
_____
_____
_____
_____
_____
_____
_____
_____
_____
_____
_____
_____
_____
_____
_____
_____
_____
_____
_____
_____
_____
_____
_____
_____

Notes

Mooneyham - Job

Notes

Ephesians 3:1–21

THE MINISTRY OF GOD'S MYSTERY
PAUL'S PURPOSE, PRAYER, AND POWER

Like most of us, I always enjoy a good mystery. I have repeatedly devoured Sir Arthur Conan Doyle's Sherlock Holmes mysteries and Agatha Christie's writings. I love a good John Grisham book. I'm always game for a good mystery movie on television or at the theater. But those are not the only sources of mysteries I find. Life itself is full of mysterious things. For example, I've heard of New Zealand, but I've never been able to find anyone who knows where Old Zealand is? And why is it that there are ten hot dogs in a pack, but the buns come in packages of either eight or twelve? And another thing—why are the hot dogs not the same length as the buns? I always hate it when you get to the end of a really good hot dog and your last bite is nothing but bread. But actually, I heard someone solved that problem and invented a "bun length" hot dog you can buy in the grocery stores. My question is "why didn't they do that to begin with?" Now, that's a mystery!

Mystery is also the theme of this third chapter of Paul's writing to the believers at Ephesus. In this week's lesson we look at the last scene of the opening act of the book of Ephesians. Paul brings to a close this wonderful treatise on defining our position in Christ. Here in chapter three Paul speaks of the mystery that Gentiles could be fellow-heirs and members of the same body with the Jews. This would, of course, be of particular interest to the Ephesian church, consisting primarily of Gentile believers. Paul received this mystery by revelation from the Lord and considered it a privilege to be a steward of these important truths.

Like the Ephesians, most of us are a part of that group called the Gentiles and we need to understand what God has done for us.

This week, we want to investigate what information Paul passes on about this mystery, because like the Ephesians, most of us are a part of that group called the Gentiles and we need to understand what God has done for us.

Ephesians 3:1-21

DAY ONE

THE REVELATION OF THE MYSTERY OF GOD (3:1–7)

Have you ever gotten up before daylight and watched a sunrise? It is an awesome thing to see the sun creeping up over the horizon as it paints the sky with a beautiful palate of red and yellow hues. I've always been fascinated with the way the murky, gray masses of objects that are concealed in the darkness slowly begin to sort themselves out into recognizable entities as daylight approaches. What once was hidden is revealed by the light. Paul speaks of a similar process, when he writes of God's uncovering of the mystery of the Gentiles. It takes God's revelation for His mysteries to be grasped. Until the church age, the mystery of the Gentiles remained hidden. But like pulling back the curtain on a drama stage, God pulls the blinders away so we can understand all He has done for us.

📖 Take some time to review the context of every verse we have studied in Ephesians thus far. Why do you think Paul begins chapter 3 with the words, *"For this reason"*?

There it is through Christ's offering and God's grace that we

are in a right relationship with God

Some translations suggest that the word "reason" in 3:1 is linked to Paul's imprisonment. According to this interpretation, Paul states that the "reason" he is imprisoned is because of his preaching to Gentile groups such as the Ephesians. Other translations read as if the word "reason" in 3:1 links Paul's revelation of the Gentile believer's position in Christ expressed in Chapter 2 to his prayers on behalf of the Ephesians. If this interpretation is correct, then Paul is stating in his opening of chapter 3 that his "reason" or purpose for praying for the Ephesians is that they know and understand their position and inheritance as Gentile believers in Christ.

Actually, Paul uses the **first two chapters** in Ephesians to reveal the Christian's newfound position in Christ, as Chapter 1 begins by listing the many things that change when one places trust in Christ. For starters, all Christians are blessed with everything in Christ (1:3), chosen in Him (1:4), adopted into God's family (1:5), and recipients of freely bestowed grace (1:6). As Christians, we are redeemed (1:7–8); receive revelation (1:8–10) and an inheritance (1:11–12). We are sealed in Christ (1:13) and receive the Spirit as a pledge (1:14). As believers, we are enlightened to God (1:15–17), to the hope of His calling (1:18), to God's possessions (1:18), to God's power (1:19–20) and to His purposes (1:21–23). Christians learn of sin's work against us (2:1–3) and of God's work for us (2:4–9), in us (2:10a), and through us (2:10b).

The main thrust, however, of Paul's *"For this reason"* statement seems to be linked to the preceding verses in Chapter 2, where he pictures the condition of Gentiles before they come to Christ (2:11–12), and most importantly, of the divine work of reconciling Jews and Gentiles (2:13–18) and unifying both ethnic groups in one body through Christ (2:13–22). Paul felt led of the Lord to unite Jewish and Gentile believers and was willing to risk imprisonment and death to see this burning desire come to fruition.

📖 Take a moment to read reflectively through the statements in verses 1 and 2 about Paul's relationship to the Gentiles and write down what you learn.

He feels responsible to bring them everything he can about the
Gospel and its blessings.

First, Paul reveals that he is a "prisoner of Christ Jesus." This could have Paul's imprisonment in view as well as his volitional choice to live his life as a "bondslave" to Christ. The addition of the phrase "for the sake of the Gentiles" seems to put the emphasis on the latter. Paul speaks of the stewardship of God's grace, given him for the sake of the Gentiles. This "stewardship" (Greek: *oikonomía,* from which our English word "economy" is derived) spoken of in verse 2 is God's entrusting Paul with the message of His grace as the apostle to the Gentiles. When Paul encountered Christ on the Damascus road, it was revealed that his specific life mission would involve taking the gospel to the Gentiles (see also Galatians 2:7; Ephesians 3:1).

📖 Read through Ephesians 3:3. What is the mystery spoken of here?

How the Gentiles and Jews can BOTH be heirs to the same
inheritance and recipients of the same promises of God

Word Study
MYSTERY

The Greek term "mystery" (*mustērion*), unlike our English word, does not mean something mysterious that cannot be understood, but rather, something previously concealed or hidden that has now been revealed to the initiated.

The "mystery" Paul speaks in verse 3 is not that the Gentiles would be blessed, although that was predicted many times in the Old Testament (Genesis 22:18; Isaiah 57:19; 60:1–4; etc.), but rather that the Gentiles and Jews would be united in one body in Christ, established as fellow heirs, and made partakers of the promise (3:6).

📖 How, according to verses 3 and 5, did Paul find out about this mystery?

Revelation direct from Christ, just as the other apostles.

Paul was enlightened to this mystery by divine revelation (3:3) as were all the apostles and prophets (3:5). The phrase "wrote before in brief" most likely does not point to another separate letter to the Ephesians, but rather to what he said in the previous two chapters. Some have suggested that this revelation occurred during Paul's "third heaven" experience that he speaks of in 2 Corinthians 12, while others view it as having occurred during his three years in the wilderness of Arabia (Galatians 1:17) shortly after his conversion.

Compare Ephesians 3:6 with 2:12 and write down the differences you observe.

> excluded from Christ → fellow partakers
> Strangers to promise → " "
> No Hope → Fellow heirs
> without God → In Christ

Before receiving Christ, the Ephesians (and all Gentiles) were separated from Christ—now they are *"in Christ."* Before, they were "excluded" (see 2:12); now they are *"fellow heirs and fellow members of the body."* Before, they were *"strangers to the covenants"*; now they are *"fellow partakers."* It is obvious that a dramatic shift in fortunes occurs for all Gentiles who place faith in Christ's redeeming work on the cross.

Take a moment to read Ephesians 3:7–8 reflectively. What do you think is the main point Paul makes?

> The biggest task is given to the "least qualified."
> Paul opposed the way as Saul. Paul is steeped in Jewish
> Tradition and law. He isn't an expert on Roman Gentile culture,
> rather on Jewish themes. To send him to the Gentiles where
> most of his knowledge about the Jewish Tradition is minimized
> simply points greater glory to God.

Here Paul gives a clear view of his ministry call, and his attitude toward it with a special emphasis on how undeserving he considered himself. First, he points out that he was "made" a minister of the gospel by God. It wasn't something he accomplished by his own striving. Second, his call was related to his spiritual gift (a *"gift of God's grace"*), not his own diligent laboring. Third, he humbly identifies himself as undeserving through representing himself as the *"very least of all saints."* (In 1 Corinthians 15:9, Paul claims he is *"the least of the apostles"* because he *"persecuted the church of God"*). He also mentions his specific call to the Gentiles (Galatians 2:7; Acts 9:15). Finally, he identifies his message to the Gentiles—a message proclaiming the incomprehensible riches of Christ.

A mystery in the spiritual sense is something that was formerly hidden but is now revealed. Paul begins chapter three of Ephesians by relating how he ended up a minister of the mysteries of God. He saw his life purpose as a person designated to uncover the mysteries of God to the Gentile world, and he thoroughly devoted himself to that cause. Paul's life as a minister was a far different career track than the one that originally consumed him. As a

Pharisee and the chief persecutor of the church, he was set on exterminating the sect called "the Way." Yet in the end, he would find himself laying his life on the line again and again trying to advance that cause.

Think about this—God chose to radically transform a religious zealot named Saul. God turned his life completely around. Then the Lord revealed to this zealot His master plan—His intention to totally change the religious structure of those who would follow Him. It is not that Saul woke up one morning, decided to change his name to Paul, and began trying to persuade Gentiles to become followers of God. No, this change was not initiated by Paul but by the Lord. It seems clear that such an alteration in direction could only come when under-girded by divine revelation. What God revealed to Paul became a compelling force in his life. But the revelation of the mystery was not merely for Paul's benefit. God revealed this powerful truth **to** Paul so that He could communicate it **through** Paul, as we will begin to see in Day Two.

The Communication of the Mystery Of God (3:8—13)

The philosopher Immanuel Kant is perhaps most famous for his treatise, *A Critique of Pure Reason*. In this book, Kant attempts to define the limits of what mankind can know with confidence. Although I don't agree with all of his conclusions, I think he brings out some interesting points about mankind. One of his main points is that we human beings are phenomenal creatures—we understand and interpret the world around us via phenomena that we can grasp through our five senses. Therefore, Kant argues, we can only really know what we can experience with the five senses: sight, smell, taste, touch, and hearing. Kant calls the realm of mankind the **"phenomenal realm."** In the phenomenal realm, according to Kant, things can be revealed to us only as they appear to our five senses. Kant teaches in his treatise that mankind cannot reach beyond this realm because he believed that our senses—the link to how things appear—form the boundary of our ability to reason. Thus Kant concludes that it is impossible for man to really know that God exists. God by His very nature, the philosopher argues, is a part of a higher realm than man. He is part of what Kant calls the **"noumenal realm,"** a dimension where things appear as they actually are—ultimate reality. To Kant, the "noumenal realm" is a level to which we human beings cannot transcend. It is too high for us. It exceeds the limits of our ability to reason only through the senses.

While I don't agree with Immanuel Kant's conclusion that it is impossible for mankind to know that God exists, there are some things I really like about his logic. First, he ascribes to the concept of God, and he ascribes to God a very high and noble place. He doesn't attempt to bring God down to the level of man. A true God whom man could fully grasp and understand with his mind through reason would be no greater than man himself. Second, I think Kant is correct in recognizing the limits of what man can grasp on his own via the confines of his faculties. Man indeed is a creature whose mind is mostly restricted to the phenomena he can grasp with the five senses.

"No one has seen God at any time; the only begotten God who is in the bosom of the Father, He has explained Him."

John 1:18

There is only one problem with Kant's conclusions. He leaves out one all-important possibility. What if God reaches down from the "noumenal realm" and reveals Himself to man in "phenomenal" ways? Man may not be able to reach God through reason, but God can reach man through revelation. That is, in fact, what God has done. He knows the limits of what man's mind can grasp. Therefore, God became a man so that mankind could understand Him. John 1:18 tells us, *"No one has seen God at any time; the only begotten God who is in the bosom of the Father, He has explained Him."* Literally, Jesus has "exegeted" God, or He has revealed God in ways mankind could understand. You see, God is knowable, but only because He chooses to make Himself known.

When we look at the mysteries of God, we must realize that they are knowable because God makes them known to us. God himself is the one who reveals. But as we look at the Holy Bible, we find that is the history of God's dealings with man. From Genesis to Revelation we have a record of God intervening and revealing Himself. God spoke through angels, through prophets, through miraculous experiences—He speaks even through creation—and, ultimately, He spoke through Jesus and further revealed Himself. The apostle Paul saw his mission in life to be the messenger of what God has revealed to those who have not heard it. He *"was made a minister"* of the mysteries of God to the Gentiles.

📖 Read Ephesians 3:8–9.

What does this say about Paul's life purpose?

To work towards the revelation of this mystery to all those that are willing to listen

Why do you think Paul adds the phrase *"who created all things"* to verse 9?

To emphasize that mystery was God's intension all along.

With great humility, Paul defines his calling to take the gospel to the Gentiles. His job was to *"bring to light"* the things hidden in God. It would seem in the immediate context, that one of those hidden things Paul is trying to bring to light is not just the mystery of God's dealings, but the *"administration"* of that mystery—not just **what** God is doing, but **how** He goes about doing it. Paul reminds them that this is the God who created all things. The apostle's intent, in light of the larger context may be to emphasize that God created all things, including the Gentiles, and not just Israel. Just because the Israelites are God's "chosen people" doesn't mean that God excludes the rest of the world from his covenantal blessing. His desire was that through His people, *"all the nations of the earth would be blessed"* (Genesis 22:18).

How is the *"manifold wisdom of God"* mentioned in verse 10 made known through the Church?

As the church administers this revelation among all humankind and brings reconciliation across the board to all who will believe, the heavenly beings can marvel at how comprehensive and full the solution to the sin problem really is!

By establishing Christ as the cornerstone of the faith, God Himself was able to make righteousness available to and through the Church—Christ's body of believers. Now, Christ's body serves as a mirror, reflecting the many-faceted wisdom of God to the angelic realm (1:21). Although God's full purpose was previously hidden (a mystery) it has, from eternity past, been His purpose to do these things.

📖 Take a moment to read and reflect on the message of Ephesians 3:11–12.

What do you think it means that we have *"boldness and confident access"*?

This is the way it is supposed to be! We don't have to feel like we sneak in the back door or anything because we don't observe the law or are descendants of Abraham.

How do we have these attributes?

Through faith in Christ

What do we do with them?

Live in relationship (positive and productive) with God

Hebrews 10:19 tells us that through the shedding of Christ's perfect blood, He purchased for us access to the "Holy of Holies"—the very presence of God. We appropriate God's presence personally as our hearts are *"sprinkled clean from an evil conscience"* (10:22) both positionally (through salvation) and experientially (as we confess and deal with sin on an ongoing basis [1 John 1:9]). Such access to God refers not only to prayer, but also to the entire communion we have with God by faith in Christ.

Just because Israel was His "chosen people" doesn't mean that God was excluding the rest of the world. His desire was that through His people, "all the nations of the earth would be blessed" (Genesis 22:18).

📖 In Ephesians 3:13, Paul exhorts these believers to not lose heart over his tribulations. Why were Paul's tribulations *"glory for the Gentiles"*?

~~They stand~~ the tribulations stand as witness to the power that God puts in Paul's life to overcome and finish strong in faith.

Word Study
APOSTLE

The English word "apostle" is a transliteration of the Greek word (*apostéllō*). It is a combination of the prefix *apó* (meaning "from") and *stéllō* ("to set, to place, to appoint to a position"). It emphasizes not just what one is sent to, but also where he is sent from. Apostles are sent forth from God.

Paul's tribulations (not just his present imprisonment, but all he endured for the gospel) were glory for the Gentiles in that through these trials he gave strong testimony to the truth of the message he both preached and lived. They were also testaments to God's great love for the Gentiles, that He would call someone to preach the good news to them at so great a cost. Paul's suffering for them gave evidence of how God saw them.

The apostle Paul was a minister of the mysteries of God. The very term, "apostle" means "one sent forth on a mission." God sent Paul to take the good news to the Gentile world and to explain the mysteries of how God was going to bring these Gentiles into the family of His people. The people who had never known God now had a man whose life purpose was to make God known to them. If that thought doesn't excite you, it is because you haven't yet grasped that it was the taking of the gospel to the Gentiles that made it possible for you and me to believe!

Ephesians 3:1–21

DAY THREE

A PRAYER FOR UNDERSTANDING (3:14—19)

Paul begins the book of Ephesians by telling the recipients of his letter that we have been blessed with *"every spiritual blessing in the heavenly places"* in Christ, and then he prayed that God might give us *"a spirit of wisdom and revelation in the knowledge of Him."* It is interesting that Paul closes out the first half of this book in much the same way he begins it—by praying for the Ephesians to understand. In verses 14—19, he prays that we may be *"able to comprehend"* God's love for us and be *"filled up with all the fullness of God."* Paul's goal for this first half of his epistle to the Ephesians has all been aimed at their understanding. Indirectly, his goal is also aimed at us today. He wants the Ephesians and all other believers to think rightly. His prayers make it clear that it is a miraculous work of God for anyone to get to the point of thinking rightly. We all need God to reveal truth to us. We need His work in our lives to move information from our heads to our hearts. This is where Paul's praying comes in. We need to understand our need for understanding. We need to grasp the fact that it is a work of God for the "eyes of our hearts" to be opened (see Ephesians 1:18). We need to trust God to enlighten us. And like Paul, we need to ask Him to do this. As you are studying, be sure that you are trusting God to reveal His all-knowing wisdom to you. Don't just try to figure things out on your own!

📖 Take a look at Ephesians 3:14 and then compare it with 3:1 and write your observations.

He is getting back to the thought he interrupted with v. 2

The almost identical wording of these verses indicates that Paul is coming back to the thought he introduced in verse 1. Verses 2–13 should be viewed as a parenthetical aside, and now Paul moves back to his original intent—to pray for the Ephesians' enablement.

In light of the context, what do you think is the significance of verse 15?

Since God is the source of everything, that includes everyone.

Here in verse 15, as in verse 9, Paul seems to be emphasizing that God is not God of the Jews only. This verse may indeed point to the fact that all mankind, good and evil, has been created by God. More likely, the verse indicates that all followers of God have been united under one name—Christ. Both Jews and Gentiles in Christ bear the name Christian, placing each group of people on common ground and equal footing.

What exactly is Paul asking for in his prayer here and why does he ask?

That we can fully give Jesus the room in our hearts to take residence there

Paul's request, distilled to its basic essence, is that the Spirit of God would fill their lives to strengthen and empower them in their walks with God. Paul follows through on this prayer in 5:18 by commanding them to *be filled with the Spirit*. Paul prays this prayer because he knows that Christ will dwell in their hearts, and he is trusting God to work in their lives to bring them to that point.

What do you think it means to be "rooted and grounded" in love (Ephesians 3:17)?

rooted – it is where we draw our sustainment, nourishment
grounded – it enables us to stand firm against when they come

Word Study
DWELL

The Greek term translated "dwell" in Ephesians 3:17 is *katoikéō* (from *katá*, [down] and *oikéō* [to dwell]) has the idea of settling down or dwelling inside. Here, it does not refer to salvation or to Christ coming into the Ephesian's hearts, but rather to Him being completely at home and in control of their lives.

Paul's metaphorical language of a tree "rooted and grounded" in love can be viewed two ways. Either he is calling for them to have a strong and firm love toward God and others, or he is pointing to God's love for them as the foundation of all they do. In light of the verses that follow, the latter seems more likely. In Revelation 2:4, Jesus rebukes the Ephesian church for having left their first love. Paul's concern for their understanding is obviously not groundless.

📖 Read through Ephesians 3:18 in the context of the verses before and after it.

Why do you think Paul prays that the Ephesians would *"comprehend"* the love of Christ?

To be able to act on it.

Why are the Ephesians supposed to comprehend Christ's love *"with all the saints"*?

as one body in unity

The Greek word used here for "comprehend" (*katalambánō*) has the idea of mentally laying hold of God's love—of fully understanding it. As we grasp the love God has for us, a greater love for God and others is generated within us. It all begins with the love of God—*"we love because He first loved us"* (1 John 4:19). This is and has been God's intent for all believers, past, present, and future.

GREAT IS THE MEASURE OF OUR FATHER'S LOVE

For as high as the heavens are above the earth, So great is His lovingkindness toward those who fear Him. As far as the east is from the west, So far has He removed our transgressions from us. Just as a father has compassion on his children, So the LORD has compassion on those who fear Him.... But the lovingkindness of the LORD is from everlasting to everlasting on those who fear Him, And His righteousness to children's children....

Psalm 103:11–13, 17

Compare verse 18 with Psalm 103:11–13, 17 and write what you see.

It is all encompassing

Paul, in verse 18, speaks of the breadth, length, height, and depth of the incomprehensible love of Christ. In Psalm 103, we see those dimensions illustrated. We see the breadth of God's love: *"as far as the east is from the west, so far has He removed our transgressions from us"* (103:12). We see the length of God's love: *"the lovingkindness of the Lord is from everlasting to everlasting"* (103:17). We see the height of God's love: *"as high as the heavens are above the earth, so great is His lovingkindness toward those who fear Him"* (103:11). Finally, we see the depth of God's love: *"as a father has compassion on his children, so the Lord has compassion"* (103:13). While I'm not saying for certain that Paul had Psalm 103 in mind as he wrote Ephesians 3, we must realize that throughout the Scriptures, God has as His goal for us to understand Him and His love for us.

📖 Read Ephesians 3:19. What do you think it means to "know" the love of Christ that surpasses knowledge?

To know as much of it as we can fathom, even though its extent moves far beyond that point (surpasses)

The word translated "know" (_ginōskō_) usually carries the idea of experiential knowledge as opposed to intuitive knowledge. In this verse, _ginōskō_ is used to convey the idea of experiencing Christ's love. Paul is praying that even though the Ephesians will never fully comprehend the love of Christ, that they would be continually deepening in their knowledge and experience of it.

How do you think that knowledge of the love of Christ fills us up to "_all the fullness of God_"?

God's love is infinite. ours can be closer to his than it was before through Christ's love.

In Galatians 5:22–23, Paul tells us that the "fruit" of the Spirit of God is love, joy, peace, patience, kindness, goodness, gentleness, faithfulness, and self-control. As we deepen in our experiential knowledge of Christ's love, these attributes of Him become manifested in us bit by bit with the end result being our glorification—when we are filled completely with the fullness of God.

Do you know that God loves you? This is the question Paul is asking in Ephesians. Paul's probing question does not stem from an idle intellectual curiosity. His desire is not just that the Ephesians know the information of God's love, but that they grasp it in their hearts. This desire applies to us as much today as it did to the church at Ephesus nearly two thousand years ago. The need to embrace the love of Christ is indeed the great need of the Church. We need to be awash in the love of God. It is a transforming truth to grasp that God loves us unconditionally. The message the people of God need to understand and then communicate to a needy world is not simply a call to morality—though that is often what religion is reduced to. As recipients of God's love, we need to become agents of that love. We need to let the world know that their Creator loves them and desires a relationship with them. We need to preach John 3:16—"_For God so loved the world, that He gave His only begotten Son, that whoever believes in Him shall not perish, but have eternal life._"

> **"For God so loved the world, that He gave His only begotten Son, that whoever believes in Him should not perish, but have eternal life"**
>
> **John 3:16**

PAUL'S POWER (3:20—21)

We live in a world that is constantly looking for new sources of energy. Fossil fuels have sustained the industrial revolution, but those fuels are not going to be around forever. The world's reserves of oil and coal are being rapidly depleted. From where will our new sources of energy come? Many in a post-Chernobyl, terrorist-threatened world do not trust nuclear power. Solar power has yet to make a significant dent in the energy consumer market. Wind power has been toyed with, but without sustained success. Where will our power come from in the new millennium? Time will tell. The apostle Paul recognized energy needs of a different nature, and he had found the solution. He had found a source of power that was inexhaustible—power for life—the power of God. He also recognized that as great as his understanding of that power was, his comprehension was inadequate, for God is *"able to do far more abundantly beyond all that we ask or think"* (Ephesians 3:20).

📖 What, according to Ephesians 3:20, is the source of Paul's power?

_____

_____

The source of Paul's power for living (and the source available to the Ephesians as well) is God, manifested in the indwelling Spirit's power working within.

What are the limits of this power Paul speaks of?

_____

_____

_____

_____

_____

Ephesians 1:19 describes God's power as *"surpassing greatness."* In Ephesians 3:20 (NASB 1995 Update), Paul repeats that concept, informing us that God is able to do *"far more abundantly beyond all that we ask or think."* God is able to do far more than we could ever imagine or would trust Him for.

What are the results of the working of that power in us (verse 21)?

_____

_____

_____

_____

_____

It is amazing to realize that, imperfect as we are, God is able to glorify Himself through us to all generations and for eternity. We were created to bring glory to God, and we find our meaning and purpose and fulfillment when God's glory is realized in us.

"Now to Him who is able to do far more abundantly beyond all that we ask or think, according to the power that works within us, to Him be the glory in the church and in Christ Jesus to all generations forever and ever. Amen.

Ephesians 3:20–21

(NASB 1995 Updated Version)

The power of God was not mere theory to the apostle Paul. He had personally experienced it. He had seen God's power radically transform his life. He had witnessed that power heal the sick and raise the dead. He had tasted of God's ability to protect him and provide for him. At one point, he even witnessed God's capability to supernaturally preserve him from death when a poisonous snake bit him. When he says, "God is able," it is not a theoretical statement, but something he had seen proven over and over again. Maybe you have not had so personal or dramatic of an experience with God's power, but you can. He is able!

FOR ME TO FOLLOW GOD

Unlike the way our culture uses the term "mystery," in the Greek culture a mystery was not something mysterious but something unknown until revealed to the person (cf. Rom. 16:25). The mystery Paul speaks of in this passage is not that Gentiles would be blessed (that was predicted in the Old Testament), but that Jews and Gentiles would be equal heirs in the body of Christ (3:6). The Jews rebelled against the idea because they wanted a position of prominence over others. God, however, has chosen to save man by grace through faith, not as a result of works (or anything else) so that no one should boast. In this way, God alone gets the glory. It is the Church's responsibility to communicate God's mysteries. Yet many times, that responsibility is neglected. The world can't understand the truths of God unless we explain them. We are "far more abundantly" rich in Christ; however, that wealth is not to be hoarded but shared with all.

APPLY The apostle Paul came to realize that his life was not to be lived for himself. When he met Christ on the Damascus road, God revealed to him that the purpose of his life was to take the good news of Christ to the Gentile world. Have you, like Paul, determined God's purpose for your life?

_____

_____

_____

_____

Have you taken time lately to thank God for the blessing of having a relationship with Him? If not, then take some time right now to praise God for who He is and all He does.

_____

_____

_____

_____

_____

Have you taken time lately to thank God for the blessing of having a relationship with Him?

APPLY Paul prayed that the Ephesians would experience God's power and understand His love. How are you doing in those areas?

_____

_____

_____

_____

Are there others you know who have need of those? If so, why not write their names down and begin praying for them regularly.

_____

_____

_____

_____

You may want to write these names on a slip of paper that you can keep tucked in your Bible as a regular reminder to be praying for them.

APPLY Man was created to bring glory to God. Are there any things in your life that the Spirit brings to mind which don't do that?

_____

_____

_____

_____

The force that short-circuits God's power in our lives is sin. The way we, as believers, can experience lives of power is through keeping short accounts with God by confessing our sins and yielding control of our lives to Him. In a world desperately in need of hope, God has called us as His light. _"Let your light shine before men in such a way that they may see your good works, and glorify your Father who is in heaven"_ (Matthew 5:16).

Why not close out this lesson by writing a prayer to the Lord, expressing your heart in the areas we talked about today…

_____

_____

_____

_____

_____

_____

_____

_____

_____

_____

_____

Notes

Notes

Ephesians 4:1-16

"Walk in a Manner Worthy"
Right Attitudes and Actions of the Christian

She had gone down in history as "America's Greatest Miser," for when she died in 1916, "Hetty" Green left an estate valued at over $100 million. She ate cold oatmeal because it cost money to heat it. Her son had to suffer a leg amputation, because she delayed so long in looking for a free clinic that his case became incurable. Hetty was very wealthy; yet she chose to live like a pauper.

Eccentric? Certainly! Crazy? Perhaps—but nobody could prove it. Hetty was so foolish that she hastened her own death by bringing on an attack of apoplexy while arguing about the value of drinking skimmed milk (from Warren W. Wiersbe, *Be Rich*, Victor Books [Wheaton, IL: 1976], p. 7). Sadly, Hetty Green is an illustration of too many Christian believers today. They have limitless wealth at their disposal, and yet they live like paupers because they don't live out their high position in Christ. It was to this kind of Christian that Paul wrote the epistle to the Ephesians.

If you studied the book of Ephesians in its original Greek language, you would find an obvious contrast between the first three chapters of Ephesians, and the last three. The first half of this wonderful book is filled with verbs in the indicative mood. These are the verbs that make simple assertions of fact. On the other hand, the second half of Ephesians is filled with verbs in the imperative mood—commands. It is the imperatives which reveal the applications Paul wants of us. The first half of Ephesians describes all of the wonderful resources we have in a

Belief always precedes behavior. We must think rightly if we are to act appropriately.

relationship with Christ, while the second half tells us what to do with those resources. The first half tells us what to believe, while the second half tells us how to behave. This is a pattern Paul follows in most of his epistles, though nowhere is it more obvious than in his letter to the church he founded in Ephesus. You see, belief always precedes behavior. We must think rightly if we are to act appropriately. On the flip side of this coin, if we think wrongly, our actions will end up being wrong no matter how sincere we are.

Ephesians 4:1-16

DAY ONE

THE RIGHT ATTITUDES IN THE BODY (4:1—2)

"Attitude is everything!" While you may not wholeheartedly embrace this slogan to the fullest extent, you certainly can agree that our attitudes are an important aspect of who we are, especially who we are as believers in the body of Christ. Our attitudes toward our fellow believers, and more importantly, our attitudes toward ourselves, must be based on truth. We must let the truths of God's word shape our attitudes and how we think. In Ephesians 4, Paul begins to help us see what proper attitudes toward others should be, and he also shows us how to get there. He guides us to *"walk in a manner worthy"* of the high calling we have in Christ (4:1). At the core of these right and proper attitudes is a concept of oneness. Paul places great emphasis on the things that serve to unite us in Christ, not those things that tend to divide us. Today we want to begin looking at these right attitudes.

📖 Ephesians 4:1 begins with the word "therefore." Look back over the main points of the first three chapters, and see if you can identify what the "therefore" is *there for* in verse 1?

This word "therefore" triggers the most significant transition in the entire book as it moves us from the first three chapters that are positional doctrine, into the final three that deal with practical duty. The word "therefore" reminds us to keep the doctrine in view as we wrestle with the duty. The last three chapters of Ephesians are filled with application. In Chapter 4, Paul doesn't just invite believers to "walk in a manner worthy," he spends the remaining three chapters telling us exactly how to do that.

Consider all the truths Paul has expressed in the previous chapters, namely His revelation of the high position which the Ephesians now held as believers. Chapter 1 begins with the many things that changed when we placed our trust in Christ: we were blessed with everything in Christ (1:3), chosen in Him (1:4), adopted into God's family (1:5), and became recipients of freely bestowed grace (1:6). We were redeemed (1:7–8); we received revelation (1:8–10) and an inheritance (1:11–12). We were sealed in Christ (1:13) and received the Spirit as a pledge (1:14). We were enlightened to God (1:15–17), to the hope of His calling (1:18), to God's possessions (1:18), to God's power (1:19–20), and to God's purposes (1:21–23). We learned of sin's work against us (2:1–3) and of God's work for us (2:4–9), in us (2:10a), and through us (2:10b). This is contrasted with what we were like before we met Christ (2:11–12), and, most importantly, of the divine work of reconciling Jew and Gentile (2:13–18) and unifying both in one body through Christ (2:13–22). In Chapter 3, Paul prays that the Ephesians might understand these truths more fully.

"I, therefore, the prisoner of the Lord, entreat you to walk in a manner worthy of the calling with which you have been called...."

Ephesians 4:1

📖 Take a look again at Ephesians 4:1.

Why do you think Paul calls himself the *"prisoner of the Lord?"*

To indicate his belief that God has him where He wants him to be.

Why do you think he mentions this here in this context?

To underline the fact that no matter the circumstances, God can use us.

When Paul calls himself the *"prisoner of the Lord,"* this may point to Paul's commitment to be a "bond-servant" of Christ (Romans 1:1). He uses that term in reference to himself in a number of his epistles. But more likely here, it is a reference to his present state, well known to the Ephesians. Paul is in prison for his witness for Christ. He may be reminding them of his imprisonment to paint a realistic picture both of what he was willing to go through to *"walk worthy"* as a model to them, and to let them know what it might cost them to walk worthy.

📖 What do you think is the purpose to which we have been called based on what Paul says in Ephesians 4:1?

Live a life that reflects our position in Christ

The Greek word translated "calling" carries the idea of a summons or a vocation. Both seem to be embodied here. There is our general calling as saints that is detailed in the first chapters of Ephesians, and there are unique individual callings related to our spiritual gifts, which Paul begins to address in this fourth chapter. His exhortation to walk worthy points as well to the one who has called us—God.

📖 Take a close look at Ephesians 4:2.

What is the main thrust of verse 2 as it relates to verse 1?

Gives the attitude with which we are to carry out our walking.

 **Word Study**
"CALLING"

The Greek term "calling" (*klēsis* [from *kaleō*, meaning "to call"]) carries the idea of a summons or a vocation. In Ephesians, we have seen our general calling as saints detailed in the first chapters, and now Paul moves into dealing with our unique individual callings related to our spiritual gifts.

How do each of the parts relate to this emphasis?

How we do it is as important as what and why.

The main verbs in verses 1–3 serve as Paul's "entreating" or urging of them to walk worthy, and these two verbs confirm the fact that they have been called. (Both verbs are found in verse 1.) The main **thrust** of verse 2 seems to define what it looks like to walk worthy. It is interesting how many "relationship" words are used in this passage. The entire meaning of the verse revolves around the central theme of relationships. *"Patience"* and *"tolerance"* are virtues we are to exhibit in all relationships. We are to exhibit patience and tolerance *"with all humility and gentleness."* Finally, *"love"* is the *modus operandi* behind our patience and tolerance for others. If we don't have Christ's love in our hearts for others, we will not possess the virtues necessary to walk in a manner worthy.

Perhaps the most important concept for us to grasp here is that God wants us to live and walk as the body of Christ, not just as a ragtag collection of individuals. As believers, we are to be connected to each other. When we function together, we become something we could never be separately. We become Christ's body here on earth—the visible manifestation of Him to those who don't know Him. The ministry that Christ carried out as an individual while He walked on earth is now the ministry of the Church.

Ephesians 4:1–16

DAY TWO

RIGHT ATTITUDES TOWARD THE BODY (4:3—6)

There is a lot of talk about unity, but it still remains an illusive concept. Some believe that unity in the body of Christ means we must all **believe** exactly the same way. Others think it means we must all **behave** in exactly the same way. But those definitions are descriptions of unison, not unity. Two cats with their tails tied together have unison, but not unity. They both have a common belief (It isn't fun being tied to another cat!) and a common objective (to get free at all cost). They both work hard toward that objective, but one could hardly say that their actions are synonymous with unity. Imagine a symphony where every instrument kept hitting exactly the same note in exactly the same way. You could describe it in one word—BORING! No, a beautiful symphony is not music in unison, but music in unity—notes that blend together to make something they couldn't make separately. This is what God wants the body of Christ to be like, and, as we see in these verses, it all begins with relationship.

📖 Read Ephesians 4:3.

What, according to verse 3, is the source of unity in the Body?

the Spirit (the same spirit) in each of us.

How is unity characterized? Where does unity originate?

As already existing, with the spirit.

Our job is to not break or mask this unity with personal desires or false teaching.

According to this verse, true unity is *"of the Spirit."* In other words, it is the logical result of having the Spirit of the living God reigning in our hearts. If the Spirit of God is ruling and reigning in my heart and in the heart of my brother, unity is automatic, for God never wars or works against Himself. When a spirit of unity exists in a group of believers, the result will be *"the bond of peace"* in the body. In Galatians 5:22, Paul identifies peace as part of the "fruit" of the Spirit.

Now, take a moment to reread Ephesians 4:3.

What do you think is meant by the exhortation to *"preserve"* unity?

It exists already as a natural extension of the Spirit in our lives.

How would that differ from us being called to **"produce"** unity?

It isn't up to us to decide the what and how of unity. Merely to accept and discard whatever disrupts it.

Often we are guilty of approaching the subject of unity in the body as if it were our responsibility to "produce" it. Verse 3 assumes unity is already there because of God. The exhortation is to "preserve" it. We can be unified with believers we have just met if the Spirit is ruling in our hearts. If He is in control, unity is automatic, for God is always one with Himself. The exhortation is to do nothing to damage that unity the Spirit is already producing.

📖 Look at Ephesians 4:4. What significance do you find in the context here of there being *"one body and one Spirit"*?

_____

_____

_____

_____

Unity is not only possible—it is to be expected, since we all as believers operate out of the position of being "one body" in Christ. Because we are one body, even though we are all gifted differently, we are interdependent (see 1 Corinthians 12:14–22). A body needs the effective operation of all its different parts. It is the one Spirit that we all share (see 1 Corinthians 12:13) that

Put Yourself in Their Shoes
UNITY

It is not our job to "produce" unity. Unity is "of the Spirit." Unity is automatic when the Spirit is in control of everyone's lives. Our job is to "preserve" the unity of the Spirit—to do nothing to disrupt the unity He is producing.

coordinates and synchronizes the corporate actions into one harmonious unit. We must realize that being filled with the Spirit is essential to the preservation of unity and harmony within the body of Christ (Ephesians 5:18).

Look again at Ephesians 4:4. What is the "one hope of our calling" to which you were called?

that Christ's sacrifice is sufficient for all.

Our corporate and individual callings both have as their aim and destiny the common hope that awaits us—to spend eternity in fellowship with our Creator in heaven. Accompanying our destination in this calling is the means to achieve it. We cannot spend eternity with God unless we become as He is—holy. Wrapped up in our calling to God is our calling to be like God—or to possess traits of Christ-likeness.

📖 Take a look at Ephesians 4:5–6. As you determine the context of these verses, what do you see as the significance of the Ephesian Church?

They are no higher, but no lower than any other Church

Paul tells us that there is one Lord, one faith, one baptism, and one God and Father "of all who is over all and through all and in all." This fact makes unity only natural. We all share common ground in each area. When Paul speaks of "one baptism," he refers not to the physical act of emersion in water, but to the spiritual act of "Spirit baptism" which occurs only once at salvation, and through which we enter the body of Christ (see 1 Corinthians 12:13).

God has done what is necessary to produce unity in the body of Christ. Our job is not to produce unity, but to preserve the unity that is already there. We must take care of our relationships and be quick to clean up our offenses. We must make right our wrongs so that the unity of the Spirit is not disrupted.

THE RIGHT PROVISION FOR THE BODY (4:7–10)

How does a human body know what to grow? Through what workings of the mortal mind does the unborn body know how to grow hands and feet or how many? By what means does it plan ears or eyes? With what strategy does it sprout arms and legs? As you know, all of these things are already mapped in the genetic blueprint. They appear as a result of the master plan. The body of Christ is built with even greater care. Jesus Christ has given each member of the body a gift—a spiritual endow-

---

Our job is not to produce unity but to preserve the unity that has already provided. We must take care of our relationships and be quick to clean up our offenses. We must make right our wrongs so that the unity of the Spirit is not disrupted.

Ephesians 4:1-16

ment to insure that the whole body is outfitted as He desires. He is the master designer—the maker of the genetic blueprint that forms the body of Christ. We don't have to figure out what to do. We simply have to relate rightly to the head of the body—Jesus.

📖 What does Paul's use of the transitional "but" in Ephesians 4:7 mean?

That although we have total unity in calling and hope we still have differences in function within the body, according to Christ's gifts.

Although we have unity because of the common bonds we share, that doesn't mean we are "clones of conformity." Because God's grace is manifested in different ways, there is a great diversity within this unity. Each of us has been gifted differently to fulfill a unique role in God's plan. This is the point of Paul's contrast.

Compare verse 7 with 1 Peter 4:10 and write your thoughts on what exactly is the "grace" that was given to "each one" of us?

the license to use the gifts we've been given

1 Peter 4:10 makes it clear every believer has been given at least one spiritual gift. When we use our giftedness, Peter indicates that we are being "good stewards of the manifold grace of God." God's grace points both to the gift and to the fact that with Christ's gift came the empowering grace to use it.

📖 What do you think is the main point of the Old Testament quote in Ephesians 4:8?

Word Study
GRACE

The Greek term for "grace" is *cháris*. The term for spiritual gifts is *chárisma*. Both Greek words share a common root; however, the suffix *–ma* indicates "the result of grace" (Spiros Zodhiates, *The Complete Word Study Dictionary New Testament*, AMG Publishers [Chattanooga, TN: 1992], p. 1471). Spiritual gifts are just that—undeserved gifts flowing out of God's grace.

The imagery in this verse seems to be speaking of one distributing the spoils of battle. It apparently is referring to the Roman military practice called a "triumph." It was their equivalent of a tickertape parade, and was an event conducted to honor outstanding military leadership in battle. The center of attention in a "triumph" was the chariot of the victorious general behind which would be chained the captured military leaders of the opposing army. Once the parade ended, the spoils of battle would be distributed as gifts. In 2 Corinthians 2:14, Paul thanks God, *"who always leads us in His triumph in Christ."* However, Scripture makes it clear that the gift Christ gives to us is to be offered back to Him in the form of service.

What do you think is meant by the statement that Christ *"descended into the lower parts of the Earth"* (4:9)?

_____

_____

_____

_____

Many take this to mean that just prior to Christ's ascension He descended into hell. However, some ancient manuscripts read "had first descended" which presents an alternate view—that in order for Christ to *"ascend on high,"* He first had to descend to Earth since He has been *"on high"* from eternity past. After close consideration, one must recognize that there is not a clear, definite, logical link with ascending on high that requires descending into hell. It seems more likely that Paul has the idea of descending to earth from heaven in mind—that is, when Paul speaks of *"the lower parts"* he is refering to Earth (as being lower than heaven), rather than using the term *"lower parts"* to refer to hell).

What do you think it means that Christ ascended *"far above all the heavens"* (4:10)?

_____

_____

_____

_____

In 2 Corinthians 12:2, Paul speaks of the "third heaven." Traditional Jewish thought divided the skies into three heavens. The first heaven, they saw as the atmosphere or the realm of the birds and clouds. The second heaven, according to the Jewish perspective, was space or the realm of the sun, moon, and stars. The third heaven, they saw as the realm where God is. The phrasing of 2 Corinthians 12:2 undoubtedly has this Jewish philosophy in view.

What an awesome picture these verses paint! Jesus conquered all our enemies—Satan, hell, and death. He returned from the grave a victor. As the victorious general, He brought back the spoils of battle and gave gifts to all His faithful subjects. The body of Christ is what it is because of His victory and His gifts.

"... so that He might fill all things."

Ephesians 4:10
(NASB 1995 UPDATED EDITION)

Ephesians 4:1–16

DAY FOUR

THE RIGHT STRUCTURE OF THE BODY (4:11–16)

Every Christian has a spiritual gift. Every believer is part of the Church, the "body" of Christ. Sometimes we look at those with particular gifts and wish we were like them. But where would the Body be if we all were the same? Where would the human body be with five noses and no ears? Where would it be with all hands and no feet? What good would it be to have three stomachs if you didn't have a heart? God has made the human body so that each part is needed. He has made the Church the same way. A body can function without ears or feet, but not as effectively. Some body parts are so essential that there would be no life without them. Yet together, these parts make something they could never be separately. A heart is useless without blood vessels. A stomach is useless without a mouth. We all are needed in the body of Christ. What a wonderful thought! What value and significance this truth places on even the most unimportant looking parts!

As one considers spiritual gifts from the vantage point of Ephesians chapter 4, it is important to recognize the flow of the passage. Verses 9 and 10 really are a parenthetical thought or aside. It is easier to grasp the flow of the passage by setting the verses off for a moment. Look at how it reads if you go directly from verse 8 to verse 11.

"Therefore it says, 'When He ascended on high, He led captive a host of captives, and He gave gifts to men.' . . . And He gave some as apostles, and some as prophets, and some as evangelists, and some as pastors and teachers."

Let's look at these gifted individuals Christ has given to the Church.

📖 Identify and explain the spiritual gifts listed in verse 11.

_____

_____

_____

_____

_____

_____

_____

_____

Paul lists five different gifted individuals here. First he mentions *"apostles"*—one sent forth. In the New Testament, this term is generally used to describe the original disciples and Paul, although it is also used in a broader sense of others (e.g., Barnabas [Acts 14:3–4]). An apostle seems to operate in the capacity of one who plants and establishes local churches, though some argue the office of apostle is no longer needed. Second, Paul mentions *"prophets."* A prophet is not necessarily one who tells the future, but rather is one who reveals the will and intent of God, hence a visionary. Third, Paul mentions *"evangelists."* An evangelist is one who declares the gospel message. (Although all are called to do this, some are specially gifted in this area.) Fourth, Paul mentions *"pastors."* A pastor is a shepherd, one who cares for the flock. Finally, Paul mentions *"teachers."* A teacher is one who instructs God's people to digest the Word of God.

Do you think this list of five different gifted individuals is an exhaustive list (explain)?

_____

_____

_____

_____

Paul's intent of listing certain gifted individuals here seems more or less to relate to spiritual gifts that equate to offices of leadership in the Church instead of telling us every different way a person can serve. More extensive lists of gifts and offices appear elsewhere. There are four passages in the New Testament which discuss the subject of spiritual gifts, and each passage looks at gifts from a different angle. Here in Ephesians 4, the emphasis is on leadership functions in the Church flowing out of gifts and the individuals who possess them. Other passages of this nature are Romans 12; 1 Corinthians 12; and 1 Peter 4.

📖 According to verse 12, what are the primary responsibilities of the congregation and the leadership in a church?

_____

_____

_____

_____

The bulk of ministry in a church is to be accomplished not by the leadership but by the laity. The leadership's responsibility is to "equip" those under their charge. First Peter 2:5 says we are all "priests." Often the work of God is greatly hindered because the leadership tries to perform the services and doesn't make adequate use of the manpower they lead.

📖 Take a look at Ephesians 4:13. What is the joint objective of leaders and laity?

_____

_____

_____

_____

_____

The end result of leadership "equipping" the laity, and of laity doing the "work of service" will be spiritual maturity in the fullest sense. The implication is that this will happen both through being ministered to and through participating in the ministry.

📖 Look at Ephesians 4:14–16. What, according to these verses, are the results of a properly operating body of believers?

_____

_____

_____

_____

"Until we all attain to the unity of the faith, and of the knowledge of the Son of God, to a mature man, to the measure of the stature which belongs to the fulness of Christ."

Ephesians 4:13

What does a healthy church look like? It looks like this. First, Paul says those in a healthy church are no longer "children" or those marked by spiritual immaturity. Rather they are marked by doctrinal stability. They aren't led astray by spiritual whims or man's trickery. Second, they speak the truth. The Greek word includes holding to or walking in the truth. Along with their truthfulness, Paul marks them as speaking the truth in love. Another characteristic of a properly operating body of believers is an evidence of Christ-likeness in every area. They grow up in every aspect into Him. It is significant that the body is fitted and held together, but it is even more significant how this is accomplished—by that which each individual part contributes. Finally, in a properly operating body of believers the body grows and builds itself up in love.

Taking Paul's statements in Ephesians 4:14–16 as a lead, reverse their order. What do they suggest will be the result if a body does not operate properly?

_____

_____

_____

_____

First, those in such a body will remain spiritual infants. (1 Corinthians 3:1–3 uses the term *"babes in Christ."*) They will be tossed about by wrong doctrine, and led astray by craftiness and deceit. They will lack of truth and/or love. Christ-likeness will be hindered. The body will become fragmented and divided. People will not be allowed to contribute. The body will not grow (quantitative) and will not be built up in love (qualitative).

The Church is called the body of Christ. According to Ephesians 4:16, this body is both fitted and held together by that which every joint supplies. Maybe you don't consider yourself a joint, but the next part of this verse makes it obvious that this idea applies to you. It says that it is the *"proper working of each individual part"* that causes the growth and building up of the body. In other words, the body of Christ won't be all it is supposed to be apart from you. You are wanted and needed.

This idea of the Church as the "body" of Christ is more than mere imagery. Think about the underlying message. When Jesus walked on earth, He was seen and heard—He made a difference. But what about today? Jesus is in heaven now, so does that mean He is no longer seen and heard? NO! Today, He is seen and heard in us! What Jesus was as an individual back then, the Church is as an entity today. When each of us plays his or her part and serves as God has gifted us under the direction of Christ the Head (verse 15), then Jesus is seen and recognized in the world today! When the parts of the body move, coordinated by the direction of the Head, needs can be met . . . ministry can happen . . . lives can be changed . . . the world can be affected.

FOR ME TO FOLLOW GOD

The desperate need of this hour, for the Church, is men and women with the "right stuff"—believers with the right attitudes toward the Body, and the right actions in the Body. One major lesson to be learned from team sports is that without teamwork you cannot win consistently. In the same way, the Church will never reach the world for Christ until we as Christians learn to operate as one body, the body of Christ. We each have a special place within the Body, a God-given spiritual ability and

"I, therefore, the prisoner of the Lord, entreat you to walk in a manner worthy of the calling with which you have been called. . . ."

Ephesians 4:1

a divine-designated role in the Church. If we fail to use our ability in fulfilling our role, then the whole Body suffers and the cause of Christ suffers. We hold a tremendous position, and with that position comes a tremendous responsibility. The following questions are meant to help you *"walk in a manner worthy of the calling with which you have been called"* (Ephesians 4:1).

 How would you rate your patience with others in the body of Christ?

usually patient ← 1 2 3 4 5 → not patient

What do you need to do differently, or how should you repent?

_____

_____

_____

_____

_____

 Perhaps one of the most profound messages of this passage is the fact that unity is not something we produce—it is something we preserve. We can't make it, but we can mess it up. What things do you do that hinder unity in the Body?

_____

_____

_____

_____

_____

Are you aware of what your spiritual gift is? If not, then take some time to seek the Lord about this. You can't be maximizing your potential if you don't know your place in the Body. We are all members of the universal body of Christ but we also need to commit ourselves to a local body of believers. Have you done this?

According to Ephesians 4:1–16 (specifically verses 11–12), there are two dynamic parts to a vibrant, healthy body of believers—leadership that equips and a laity that builds up the body. Do you have a leader who equips you? (If not, then begin pursuing such a member.)

Are you actively involved in building up the body you are a part of? (If not, why not?)

_____

_____

_____

_____

_____

_____

The message of this section of Ephesians has the potential to be life-changing (and certainly Church-changing). Why not seal off the applications you want to see in your life by writing out a prayer to the Lord?

_____

_____

_____

_____

_____

_____

_____

_____

_____

_____

_____

_____

_____

_____

_____

Notes

Ephesians 4:17-32

Out of the Darkness
Modeling Your Life after Christ

Walking in darkness can be a frustrating and danger-ous thing. I say this from personal experience. In 1994, our church did an outreach program on the crucifixion of Christ at a local auditorium. In just a few days, we were able to expose more than ten thousand people to the gospel. It was a great success. But part of our agreement with the auditorium management meant that we had to tear down our set and clear everything out within twenty-four hours of the program's finish to make room for the next event. Hundreds of people volunteered, and that morning was a beehive of activity. I spent most of the morning working in the basement of the center packing props and set materials. When my job was finished, I decided to head up to the stage to see if they needed my help. Being unfamiliar with the layout of the building, I wandered down hallways in the general direction I thought I should head. I found it wasn't easy to move directly up to stage level. As I was walking down a hall, I saw a sign on the door that said "Orchestra Pit." I reasoned in my mind that this should be a quick way to get up to the stage. The first door placed me in a small unlit alcove with another door on the other side. I opened the second door into the orchestra pit and found it pitch black. I reached around to the side to find a light switch, and the next thing I knew, I was falling.

Falling in the dark is not a pleasant experience, but it is made still worse when you have time to think, "I'm still falling!" Three stories later I landed on my side on a concrete floor.

Walking in darkness can be a frustrating and dangerous thing.

Amazingly, I never lost consciousness, but I had enough pain to realize I was seriously injured. My left arm was shattered and wouldn't work. I could feel blood dripping down my hand. The pain in breathing made it obvious I had broken some ribs though I was unsure how many. And I was still in the dark. As I stood to my feet, I could faintly see light under the door I had stepped through three stories above. As I felt my way around the room, I soon realized there was no exit on the level where I was standing. I was actually one floor below the basement level. I tried calling for help, but it is hard to yell very loud when you have broken ribs. As I became acclimated to my surroundings and my eyes adjusted to the darkness, I could tell that I was in a room the size of the orchestra pit, and in the middle were two hydraulic poles on which the pit could be raised and lowered. Apparently the pit had been raised to stage level for moving materials, and I had tried to enter it at normal level through a door inadvertently left unlocked. I had fallen under the pit. Then it hit me. "What if they lower the orchestra pit down?"

I could see a doorway one floor above where I stood, but there was no way to reach it. For about an hour I waited, yelled, and paced the floor. In a corner I found a broom and began banging it against the door above me. At that moment, the supervisor of the teardown project happened to be walking down that same hallway making a last check of the building before everyone left. Thankfully he heard me. Quickly keys to the door were found and a ladder was brought in to get me out. A bumpy ambulance ride strapped to a backboard wasn't much fun with seven broken ribs. But I was safe. Only after I sat in the hospital emergency room and explained all that happened did I realize how close I came to paralysis or death. It took eight hours of surgery to put my arm back together, and, to this day, I cannot completely straighten it. But I am thankful things were not worse. I had shattered one arm and broken the other wrist. In addition to the broken ribs, I had ruptured my kidney, but amazingly that was all. In the intensive care ward with me were two others who had fallen from about the same height. One had brain damage and the other lost a leg. After a year of therapy, I have most of the use of that arm back, and only scars as reminders that it is dangerous and foolish to walk in darkness.

Many people today walk in spiritual darkness. Many who now believe spent years in that darkness. When I came to faith in Christ as a young adult, it was truly as if someone had turned the lights on. But Christianity isn't just seeing the light, its walking in the light. This week's passage focuses on walking in the light we have. You see, the Bible wasn't written just to be studied but to be obeyed.

Ephesians 4:17-32

DAY ONE

THE ADMONITION TO WALK IN LIGHT (4:17—19)

Imagine what it would be like the day after Jesus raised Lazarus from the dead if Lazarus disappeared and his sisters found him back in the tomb. Imagine the conversation.

"Come on back to the house," says Martha. "There is work to be done."

"What are you doing hanging out here?" Mary chimes in.

"I dunno," replies Lazarus, "I'm kind of used to it here in the tomb—after all, I spent three days here. After a while you get used to the darkness, and the smell kind of grows on you." We would find it inconceivable that he would go back to the tomb and put back on the grave clothes after having been raised from the dead. What would death have to offer after regaining life? Yet sadly, though we have been raised from spiritual death, sometimes Christians go back to hanging out in the tombs of worldly sins and wearing the fleshly garments of the old man. It is sort of like a caterpillar who becomes a beautiful butterfly but still crawls around instead of flying. We have been given a new life in the light. Paul says we have no business going back to the darkness.

📖 Read through Ephesians 4:17 and then compare it with 2:1–3. How do the Gentiles walk?

_____

_____

_____

_____

_____

Paul exhorts us that we should no longer walk as the Gentiles (or unbelievers) walk. As we look back at chapter 2, we get a sense of how unbelievers walk. First, they are dead toward God. There is no spiritual life in them. They walk in bondage in their trespasses and sins according to the course of the world—the present system that is influenced by the enemies of God. They live according to Satan in disobedience to God's will and way, enslaved in the lusts of the flesh and incapable of changing. Their nature is to be "children of wrath" (see Lesson 4). Paul admonishes the Ephesians (and us) not to walk that way. We have been freed from that prison and should not go back to its chains.

What do you think it means in 4:17 that unbelievers walk *"in the futility of their mind"*?

_____

_____

_____

_____

The Greek word for futility (literally "vanity") carries the idea of worthlessness or nothingness. Matthew Poole in his Bible commentary states, ". . . their minds themselves, and understandings, the highest and noblest faculties in them being conversant about things empty, transient, and unprofitable, and which deceive their expectations . . . therefore are vain." That which is not eternal is eternally out of date and therefore is futile, no matter how temporarily pleasurable or desirable it may seem. Futility captures the way of the unbeliever.

> "So this I say . . . that you walk no longer just as the Gentiles also walk, in the futility of their mind."
>
> Ephesians 4:17

> That which is not eternal is eternally out of date and therefore is futile, no matter how temporarily pleasurable or desirable it may seem.

📖 Read through Ephesians 4:18 and answer the questions that follow.

What do you think it means that they are *"darkened in their understanding"*?

_____

_____

_____

_____

Do you think it is fair that they are *"excluded from the life of God"* because of ignorance?

_____

_____

Where do you think the *"hardness of their heart"* fits in to this prospect?

_____

_____

_____

_____

The unbeliever walks without light. While at a glance it may seem harsh that they are excluded from the life of God because of their ignorance, they deserve to be excluded from the life of God because their ignorance is willful ignorance. As the epistle says in 4:18, their ignorance is *"because of the hardness of their heart."* God rejects them because they have rejected Him. Romans 1:21 tells us *"For even though they knew God* [through what He had revealed of Himself in creation]*, they did not honor Him as God or give thanks, but they became futile in their speculations, and their foolish heart was darkened."* In other words, they were darkened in their understanding because they rejected God and hardened their hearts toward what He had revealed of Himself. Ignorance is not sin, but willful ignorance is.

📖 What, according to verse 19, is the reason for impurity?

_____

_____

_____

_____

When we become callous or allow our hearts to become hard and insensitive to God, sins governed by sensuality become easy choices to make. We give ourselves over to sensuality as we seek an alternate way to be fulfilled, but as we make these poor choices and reject God's will and way for our lives, God must respond as well. Romans 1:24–32 indicates that dishonor, degradation, and depravity are God's indictments on those who reject Him.

Colossians 1:13 tells us God has *"rescued us from the domain of darkness, and transferred us to the kingdom of His beloved Son."* We have been shown the light. We need not walk in darkness anymore.

THE ARGUMENT FOR WALKING IN THE LIGHT (4:20—24)

Over the course of your lifetime, you probably have stubbed your toes enough times to be convinced of the need to turn the lights on when you walk through your house. I have often thought that the main reason God gave us toes was for finding furniture at night. But for whatever reason, we still sometimes find ourselves stumbling in the dark instead of walking in the light. In verses 20–24 Paul builds his case for why we ought to walk God's way instead of our own. It is always important to answer the "why" questions along with the "what" questions. As the philosopher Friedrich Nietzsche said, "If a man has a 'why' he can overcome almost any 'how.'" Today we want to examine Paul's arguments for walking in the light.

> "If a man has a 'why' he can overcome almost any 'how.'"
>
> — Friedrich Nietszche

📖 Take a moment to reflect on Ephesians 4:20–21. What do you see as the meaning of these verses?

_____

_____

_____

_____

_____

_____

When Paul says, *"But you did not learn Christ in this way,"* his message seems to be that the Ephesians did not learn the doctrine of Christianity (which cannot be separated from the person of Christ), leading them to participating in the types of sinful behavior of which Gentiles commonly participated. If one truly knows Christ and is growing in Him, he or she must be moving toward a life and walk which is consistent with Christ's character. Otherwise, such a person is self-deceived and is not truly following Christ. As this passage points out, "*. . . truth is in Jesus.*" If one's walk isn't resulting in Christlike character, then it must be doubted if they are really walking in truth.

📖 Why, according to verse 22, should we *"lay aside the old self"*?

_____

_____

_____

_____

_____

_____

We should lay aside the old self, because it is *"being corrupted in accordance with the lusts of deceit."* In other words, the longer you live, the more corrupt the "old self" (literally "old man") becomes. As the old man becomes more corrupt, it costs us more to allow him to be in control. Hebrews 3:13 warns us that this *"deceitfulness of sin"* will harden our hearts if left unchecked.

📖 Read Ephesians 4:23. What do you think it means to be *"renewed in the Spirit of your mind"*?

_____

_____

_____

_____

> "The only way to keep a broken vessel full is to keep the faucet running."
>
> D. L. Moody

To be *"renewed in the spirit of your mind"* is not a point of enlightenment, but rather a continual process or gaining God's perspective through meditating on His word. Perhaps this phrase is better translated, "**being** renewed in the spirit of your mind," for the Greek verb is in the present tense, meaning continuous action. The "spirit" referred to here is most likely not the Holy Spirit but rather the mental and emotional make up of the person—or that person's "spirit" within. Our minds—our way of thinking—have been stained by our own fleshly nature and this fallen world in which we live. We must immerse ourselves in God's Word in order to continually gain a new way of thinking. As the great evangelist D. L. Moody used to say, "The only way to keep a broken vessel full is to keep the faucet running."

📖 Read through Ephesians 4:24.

How do we *"put on the new self"*?

_____

_____

_____

_____

Why do we do this?

_____

_____

_____

_____

Here in this verse, as in verse 22, Paul speaks metaphorically of our spiritual state as clothing or as a garment. Before salvation all we possessed were the filthy rags of sin, and thus had no choice but to wear them. At salvation, we were fitted with holy and righteous garments ("clothed with Christ") called the "new self" (literally "new man"), yet in order to wear them experientially we must take off the old garment and put on the new. We must "lay aside" the rags of the old man (through confession and repentance) and "put on" the new garment (through yielding and trusting). In light of the resulting fruit, we should certainly desire to do so.

What is the significance in verse 24 of the statement *"in the likeness of God"*?

_____

_____

_____

_____

The phrase *"in the likeness of God"* (literally translated "according to God") points to the obvious consistency between God and the new man He creates in us (2 Corinthians 5:17). It was God's intent from the very beginning for man to reflect His image in the world. When sin entered into the picture, that image of God in man was marred and distorted. In essence, what God is accomplishing by "clothing us with Christ" is re-creating man in the image of God that he might once again reflect his Creator to the world.

We have new clothes—beautiful, spotless garments. Yet, amazingly, we sometimes figuratively wear the filthy rags of our old, fallen existence. Just as the literal clothing we put on each day is a choice, so too are the spiritual garments we wear. What Paul is calling us to is a lifestyle of consistently dressing in the new garments of Christ—clothing ourselves in righteousness and holiness.

PRACTICAL OUTWORKING OF THE NEW GARMENT (4:25—29)

Some look at the Christian faith as a set of outmoded, outdated religious beliefs of days gone by. But nothing could be further from the truth. In fact, the message of Christ is incredibly practical to everyday living. God who created us and the lives we enjoy, knows how best this life should be lived. His will for our lives is not meant to restrict, but to provide and protect. His garments are so much better to wear than our own. Still He leaves the choice to us as to what we will wear each day.

📖 In the light of verse 24, what do you think is the significance of the exhortation in verse 25?

_____

_____

_____

_____

_____

The word "therefore" always marks a transition. In this case, Paul is shifting from the doctrine of verses 22–24 into the practical applications of how to live that doctrine out. The first application, mentioned here in verse 25, is that since truth is an integral part of the character of God, it should be reflected in our speech and in our relationships.

📖 Explain, in your own words, verses 26 and 27 and how you think they relate to each other.

_____

_____

_____

_____

Doctrine

GIVE PLACE TO THE DEVIL

Ephesians 4:27 indicates that unresolved anger can "give a place" to the devil. Some have argued that this passage means a Christian can make room for demonic influence in his life. The Greek word translated "opportunity" (*tópos*—from which we get our English term "topography") can refer to a literal place or can be used figuratively. If it is taken literally, this "place" should be seen as making room for the devil in our relationships, not an actual physical place within our bodies.

In God's system, there is a legitimate place for "righteous anger" such as was exhibited by Christ in the Temple (see Luke 19:45–48), but we must be wary as this "righteous" attitude can easily give way to unrighteous attitudes such as bitterness, jealousy, or a critical, judgmental spirit—thus giving the devil an opportunity (literally "a place"). This verse presents clear-cut criteria for discerning whether or not our anger is justified, as righteous anger is resolved by day's end and unrighteous anger is not.

📖 Identify and explain the significance of the contrast in verse 28.

_____

_____

_____

_____

_____

_____

Again, Paul continues his illustrations of this "put off/put on" principle as it applies to daily living. In this instance, the person is exhorted to lay aside the old manner of life (which in this case involves providing for his needs by stealing) and take on a new lifestyle of working, not only to provide for his own needs but to be able to share with others in need—becoming a giver instead of a taker.

📖 Take a look at Ephesians 4:29. How does this say our speech fits in with the process of "laying aside" the old self and "putting on" the new?

_____

_____

_____

_____

_____

_____

The Greek word translated "unwholesome" in this verse is literally "rotten," which would certainly be in keeping with the old self, not the new. Part of living out our new life involves speech that is edifying (that builds up), that meets present needs, and that "gives grace" (either conversation that spreads God's grace or gracious conversation that gives to others as opposed to that which is self-centered).

We cannot imitate Jesus, but we can yield to Him and let Him live His life through us.

We are beginning to see the threads of the new garments weaved together into a beautiful, multicolored pattern of the character of Christ. The clothing of righteousness that God wants us to wear reveals practically what Jesus would do in the everyday situations of life. It is so important that we understand the central message of 4:17–29. Paul is not saying that we should grit our teeth and try hard to be like Jesus. What he is saying is that we should put Jesus on like a garment so that He is seen instead of us. We cannot imitate Jesus, but we can yield to Him and let Him live His life through us. When we do this, we are putting on the new garment of Christ and taking off the old garment of self.

THE PRACTICE OF THE NEW
(EPHESIANS 4:30–32)

Here in Ephesians 4, the apostle Paul tells us about the new clothing that is ours to wear. He exhorts us to "pull it off the hanger" each morning and make it our chosen attire. What is this new garment? It is Jesus. Paul has shown us how to *"put on the Lord Jesus,"* but now he shows us even further. Not only does he show us how to put on the new garment, he also shows us the types of actions that take this garment off and replace it with the dirty rags of "the old man." The application Paul desires is obvious; however, the choice is ours. What will we wear today?

📖 In Ephesians 4:30, Paul commands us not to *"grieve the Holy Spirit."* How does the context indicate we might do that?

_____

_____

_____

_____

Scripture speaks of several ways we can resist and rebel against the Spirit of God dwelling in us. Here it speaks of "grieving" the Holy Spirit. This very human term helps us identify with the consequences of our sins. The context indicates God is grieved inwardly—pained—when we speak out of the old life instead of speaking words of grace and edification.

There are three main passages that speak directly to our relationship to the Holy Spirit. Here we see the possibility of "grieving" the Spirit by what we do. These acts are sins of **commission**—things we do that we shouldn't. In 1 Thessalonians 5:19 we see that we "quench" the Spirit by what we don't do. These acts are sins of **omission**—when we omit acts of obedience. In Acts 7:51, we see that if we aren't surrendered we can end up "resisting" the Spirit while thinking we are serving God. This type of sin would be a sin of **submission**—not submitting ourselves to the Lord's reigning in our hearts.

📖 How do we *"put away"* the actions and attitudes mentioned in verse 31?

_____

_____

_____

_____

Each of the actions and attitudes mentioned in this verse are part of the "old self" mentioned in verse 22 and must be "laid aside" as an act of the will. In order to experience consistent victory in the areas where we struggle, we must not only lay it aside, but we must also "put on" the new self by yielding these areas to Christ's control and expressing our dependence on Him. Part of a long-range plan for victory must also be cultivating a renewed mind—through Bible study and counsel and learning to view those problem areas from God's perspective.

Did You Know?

❓ THREE TYPES OF SIN

- **sins of commission—** doing what we shouldn't
- **sins of omission—** not doing what we should
- **sins of submission—** doing our own thing

Take another look at Ephesians 4:31. Explain in your own words as best you can the meaning of each of these attitudes and actions.

Bitterness

_____

_____

_____

Wrath

_____

_____

_____

Anger

_____

_____

_____

Clamor

_____

_____

_____

Slander

_____

_____

_____

Malice

_____

_____

_____

Let's look at the terms Paul applies to the old garment needing to be taken off:

1) **Bitterness**—abiding resentment and blame that is directed toward someone, it is the opposite of grace (see Hebrews 12:15)

2) **Wrath**—(Greek: *thumos,* from which our English prefix "thermo" [heat] is derived) has the idea of a sudden boil-over of emotions

3) **Anger**—(Greek: *orge,* from which our English word "orgy" is derived) originally meant any human emotion and came to be associated with anger which was considered the strongest of human passions. An *orge* of anger would be a full indulgence in the emotion

4) **Clamor**—seems to carry the idea of verbal expression of anger

5) **Slander**—the Greek word used here is the one we transliterate "blasphemy," though here it probably means to speak evil of a person as opposed to speaking evil of God

6) **Malice**—(literally "evil") the catch-all term to wrap up this area—in other words, "put away these evils along with any other evils I failed to mention."

📖 Read Ephesians 4:32. Why do you think we are encouraged to forgive *"just as God in Christ also has forgiven"* us?

_____

_____

_____

This verse, reminiscent of the Lord's Prayer (*"forgive us . . . as we forgive"*) calls us to reflect God in this critical area of forgiveness. All of us stand in need of God's grace and forgiveness. What a cruel injustice it is when we who are so needy of forgiveness from God, withhold forgiveness from others (Matthew 18:21–35).

What is the essential application of this last half of Ephesians chapter 4? First, we are called to lay aside the old life (4:22). This concept is not referring to salvation only since the epistle was written to believers. Second, we are asked to cultivate a renewed mind (4:23)—gaining a new way of thinking as we see life from God's perspective through His word. Finally, Paul calls us to "put on" the new self (4:24), which is Christ. As we have walked through the entire passage, we have seen a series of applications to this call. What marks this passage is a constant moving back and forth between what we are to put off and what we are to put on in terms of our Christian living. This is what walking in the light of God's word is all about.

FOR ME TO FOLLOW GOD

What a cruel injustice it is when we who are so needy of forgiveness from God, withhold forgiveness from others.

Ephesians 4:17-32
DAY FIVE

One of the most widespread misconceptions of Christianity is the idea that it is nothing more than "fire insurance." Many people believe that as long as they have trusted Christ at some point in their lives, then they don't have to go to hell—after all, all Christianity is supposed to do is to keep folks out of the flames of hell. In reality, however, if we genuinely place our trust in Christ, then we can't go on with business as usual. Our decision to trust Christ should radically affect every area of our lives. Jesus said *"I come that they might have life, and might have it abundantly"* (John 10:10). If Jesus can give us a full and meaningful life, then living life His way will be the most satisfying life possible. Paul, in this last half of Chapter 4, makes it clear the Christian life is very different than the old life. The following questions should prove helpful as you evaluate your own spiritual condition and consider what changes are necessary as you "lay aside" the old self and "put on" the new.

 Here in Ephesians chapter 4, Paul emphasizes the need to change our thinking. What are some areas the Lord brings to mind where your thinking needs to be changed?

_____

_____

_____

One of the most practical ways we can cultivate a renewed mind is by meditating on Scripture. List some problem areas in your life.

_____

_____

_____

_____

_____

_____

Now locate some passages that relate to these problem areas and set aside some time to meditate on them regularly.

_____

_____

_____

_____

APPLY Have you ever seriously laid aside the old self and given it to God? (if not, why not?)

_____

_____

_____

_____

The Holy Spirit is grieved or pained by sin, especially sins of the tongue. Jesus made it clear that the mouth speaks out of that which fills the heart. What does your speech reveal about your heart?

_____

_____

_____

It is the Holy Spirit's job to convict us of sin. As you close out this week's lesson with a written prayer to the Lord, ask God to make you sensitive to Him as you review the sins Paul mentioned.

_____

_____

_____

_____

_____

_____

_____

"The thief comes only to steal and kill and destroy; I came that they may have life, and have it abundantly."

—Jesus Christ in John 10:10

Notes

Notes

Ephesians 5:1-17

WALKING IN THE LIGHT
LIVING IN THE LIGHT OF GOD'S LOVE

Have you ever thought about what it means that the Christian life is called a walk? Philosopher Soren Kierkegaard called the Christian faith a blind leap of faith. But that is not scriptural terminology. Nowhere does the Bible call the faith a leap—it calls it a walk. Think about it. What is a walk? It is a lot of little steps in the same direction. It is a journey taken one step at a time. That is what we are called to—a walk. The word "walk" appears some 233 times in the New American Standard translation of the Bible (NASB). The vast majority of those times it is used to refer to our pursuit of God and our relationship with Him. The word "leap" is used nine times, but none in reference to our relationship with the Lord. When you think about the cultural picture that paints, it speaks of journey, but it also speaks of fellowship. In the culture of the Bible, walking was the main means of transportation. But rarely did one walk alone. Often a journey was used not simply to get from one place to another, but also to spend time with someone else. Unhurried conversations and times of personal reflection marked this mode of travel. A journey such as this is what God invites us to—a journey to the destination of eternity. But there is purpose in the trip, not just in the arrival. God wants us to converse with Him through life. He wants to use our travels to cross our paths with others who will join in the journey.

So how does God want us to walk this walk of the Christian life? This last half of Ephesians is all about living out the faith

> *What is a walk? It is a lot of little steps in the same direction. It is a journey taken one step at a time.*

the first three chapters has explained. One thing that ought to be standing out to you already is how many time the word "therefore" appears in this latter section. It appears three times in chapter 4: verses 1, 17, and 25. It also appears three more times in the verses we will study today in Chapter 5. In verse 1 Paul says, *"Therefore, be imitators of God."* He tells us how to walk with God. In verse 7, after speaking of those who do not imitate Him, Paul says, *"Therefore do not be partakers with them."* He tells us how not to walk with God. In verse 15 he writes, *"Therefore be careful how you walk,"* and exhorts us to walk wisely. What is the bottom line? God wants us to walk with Him through life.

Ephesians 5:1-17

DAY ONE

WALKING IN LOVE (5:1—6)

There is a tendency in spiritual circles to think that others (and therefore, God) should be impressed by how much we know. Information equals godliness and spiritual value. We might not say it in those terms, but this terse message is preached loudly by how we live. Another tendency is to think that others (and therefore, God) should be impressed by how gifted and talented we are. Giftedness equals importance is the unspoken message here. But neither of these messages in themselves are affirmed by the Bible. In fact, it is quite the opposite. James tells us that we should prove ourselves doers of the Word and not merely hearers "who delude themselves." In layman's terms, knowledge alone deludes us or deceives us into thinking we are spiritual because of how much we know instead of how we live. In 1 Corinthians 8:1 Paul wrote, *"Knowledge makes arrogant, but love edifies."* The apostle Paul spoke extensively of spiritual giftedness in 1 Corinthians 12, but he closed out the chapter by saying, *"and I show you a still more excellent way,"* and spent the whole next chapter talking about love. Do you get the point? Love is what really matters in the Christian life.

📖 What do you see as the point of the connective "therefore" in Ephesians 5:1?

_____

_____

_____

_____

In the book of Ephesians, chapters 1—3 were almost entirely devoted to doctrine. These last three chapters are made up of a series of "therefores," indicating application of doctrinal teaching in increasing clarity. Certainly the "therefore" here in verse 1 links Chapter 5 with Chapter 4 and brings it into a clearer, more specific focus, but both are applications of the positional truths of the first three chapters.

📖 Read through Ephesians 5:1–2. In what way are we to be imitators of God?

_____

_____

_____

_____

118 FOLLOWING GOD – THE BOOK OF EPHESIANS

First, Paul tells us we are to imitate God *"as beloved children."* Children imitate their parents because they follow them, respect them, and love them. Paul points out that one of the specific ways we are to imitate is by *"walking in love."* In this we can walk, following Christ's example, who loved us and gave Himself up for us. In this sense, we are imitators of God when we give up our rights for the sake of benefiting others. Finally, we should imitate Christ in offering our lives as a sacrifice to God—something well pleasing that smells sweet to Him.

What, according to verse 1, should motivate us to be imitators of God *"as beloved children"*? The most powerful motivation in our walks with God is His love—His unconditional favor toward us. Thirty years after this was written, this same group of believers would be rebuked for leaving their first love, and warned of losing their ministry as a result (see Revelation 2). It is God's love for us that draws us to Him.

Think about what you have seen in verses 1–2. What is the significance of Christ's example as mentioned in verse 2?

_____

_____

_____

_____

_____

Chapter 4, and now chapter 5, indicates that our aim is to imitate God, yet it is difficult for a human to imitate God who is also spirit. We don't see God face temptation, endure trials, pray, or study the Scriptures. Yet when God became flesh and dwelt among us, He showed those to us and much more. That is why Christ's example is so essential to us being able to imitate God.

📖 Take a look at Ephesians 5:3. Why is the warning in verse 3 so important?

_____

_____

_____

_____

Paul exhorts that immorality (sexual) and impurity and greed not even be named among believers. This challenge seems reminiscent of Paul's exhortation to *"Abstain from all appearance of evil"* in 1 Thessalonians 5:22 (KJV). In light of our identity as *"beloved children"* our actions are not a reflection on us only but on our heavenly Father as well. We are to accurately reflect Him to a world that doesn't know Him.

📖 Look at Ephesians 5:4. What do you think is the meaning and significance of the contrast here in this verse?

_____

_____

_____

_____

Word Study
FREEWILL OFFERINGS

The Greek word for "offering" (*prosphorá*) used in Ephesians 5:2 speaks of offerings consisting of products from the fields and trees used not for sin, but for freewill offerings. The word for "sacrifice" was used of the offering of animals which were killed and offered on the altar in atonement for sins.

Much like the contrasts of chapter 4, this verse serves to illustrate the difference in lifestyle (specifically here in the area of speech) between the old man and the new. The term, *"filthiness"* has the meaning of obscene, filthy communication. *"Silly talk"* (literally *"foolish talking"*) speaks of foolish, meaningless speech, unprofitable to those who hear. *"Coarse jesting"* is similar to the previous—yet in an exaggerated, negative way. Such jesting is not only unprofitable, but also damaging. Some take the term "coarse" to link the words *"coarse jesting"* with sexual innuendo, but the Greek word that is translated *"coarse"* in this verse is not that specific. The main idea of verse 4 is that our mouths should be used for giving thanks (profitable talk) instead of profitless, damaging speech.

📖 Read through Ephesians 5:5–6 reflectively and answer the questions that follow.

What is Paul's point in verses 5 and 6?

_____

_____

_____

_____

What impact do these verses have on salvation by grace through faith?

_____

_____

_____

_____

Word Study

IMMORAL CONDUCT

The Greek word for "immoral" in Ephesians 5:5 is *pórnos,* from which we get our term "pornography." It specifically points to sexual immorality and often was used in association with one who prostitutes themselves for personal gain.

Paul is not teaching that to go to heaven one must never sin, nor is he teaching that Christians who commit any of these sins he mentions will lose their salvation. Both would contradict the teaching of Scripture in many other places. Rather, his point seems to be that since these are the lifestyle characteristics of one who rejects God ("sons of disobedience"), they shouldn't be allowed to even make a brief appearance in the life of the believer (see 5:3).

How are we to walk with God? The main point here is not simply that we avoid moral sins. Christianity is far more than simply a list of rules to follow. The main point is that we walk as children—in relationship with God. What motivates us toward holiness is not fear of God's wrath, nor is it the hope of earning favor. Because we love God, we want to please Him with the way that we live. Most of all, we want to be like Him.

Ephesians 5:1–17

DAY TWO

WALKING IN THE LIGHT (5:7—10)

The other day my wife walked into the room where I was writing and exclaimed, "Why don't you turn some lights on!" It wasn't until she said this that I realized it had gotten quite dark in the room as evening approached. The change had been so gradual that I didn't really notice it. But once the lights were turned on, I realized how much better I could see. As I walk with God in this fallen world, I am amazed at how dark it is becoming. I look at the dialogue and situations that are commonplace on television today that would have never been tolerated when I was a child. But television entertainment is merely reflecting the changing values of our culture. America cannot fairly be called a "Christian nation" anymore. The other day my son wanted to go see a movie, and sadly there was nothing to be seen except PG-13 or R rated movies. It has become rare to find a PG movie, let alone anything rated G anymore. Our world is getting darker, and that makes it more important than ever for believers to walk in the light of God's Word. I applaud you for taking the effort to study His Word. You are shining light into your life!

📖 Read over Ephesians 5:7. Why are we exhorted not to be "partakers" with those mentioned in verses 5 and 6?

_____

_____

_____

_____

We are not to be *"partakers"* with those who follow the ways of the world, even though in our unregenerate state we were *"darkness"* just as they are at present. But now we are *"light"* like our heavenly Father (1 John 1:5) in whom there is *"no darkness at all."* Again, the application Paul calls us to here is obvious—a proper response of gratitude, for all of God's favor is to walk like Him as His child.

APPLY Verse 8 says *"you were formerly darkness."* What are some of the dark things that characterized your life before you met Christ?

_____

_____

_____

_____

_____

Depending on how young you were when you became a Christian, you may or may not have a very long list. Remember that the Ephesians were not raised to be religious. They were Gentiles who came to Christ through the missionary efforts of the apostle Paul and had not been believers for very long. One of the things we learned of them in looking at the book of Acts was that witchcraft was very prominent in that culture, and many occultic books were burned as a result of the church's growth there.

📖 Compare Ephesians 5:8 with 2 Chronicles 31:20–21. If we are walking *"as children of light"* what will that look like?

_____

_____

_____

_____

"For you were formerly darkness, but now you are Light in the Lord; walk as children of Light. . . ."

Ephesians 5:8

In this passage, as in 2 Chronicles 31, the fruit of the Father of light is described as *"goodness"* (a general virtue as opposed to wickedness), *"righteousness"* (right standing—fulfilling that which is right), and *"truth"* (as opposed to error, lies, and hypocrisy). The term, "children of light" is an Hebraism (a cultural expression) meaning "those who are in a state of light, or enlightenment (see Ephesians 1:18–20), endued with knowledge and holiness" (according to *Matthew Henry's Bible Commentary,* vol. 6, p. 711).

📖 If we are walking in the light, what does verse 10 indicate will be our attitude toward God?

_____

_____

_____

_____

To walk in the light requires an attitude much like David (a man *"after God's own heart"*), of *"trying to learn what is pleasing to the Lord."* The light versus darkness theme is one of the most practical applications of the entire epistle of Ephesians. If we cultivate this application into a heart attitude then God is honored even in our imperfection.

Years ago, I had the opportunity to share a meal with the great revivalist, Major Ian Thomas, founder of Ravencrest Bible Institute in Estes Park, Colorado. He was a man for whom I had great respect and whose teachings on the exchanged life I had found extremely helpful in my walk. Toward the end of the meal I asked, "Major Thomas, do you have any advice to offer a young man like myself who is new in the ministry?" He responded quickly, "Please Christ." He must have seen the disappointment on my face. I was expecting something more profound and practical. He explained, "Eddie, if you focus on pleasing Christ, everything else will take care of itself." The advice has never left me, and the older I get the more profound and practical I find it to be. A life of pleasing Christ is what Paul calls us to here.

> *"Please Christ. . . . If you focus on pleasing Christ, everything else will take care of itself."*
>
> *—Major Ian Thomas*

DON'T WALK IN DARKNESS ANYMORE (5:11–14)

The scene is more than a quarter of a century old, but it is still etched in my mind as if it were yesterday. A knock on my dormitory door revealed one of my drug buddies with an invitation. "Hey Eddie, we are getting ready to smoke some pot—want to join us?" A look of incredulity spread across his face as I replied, "You know, I don't think I'm going to do that anymore." I'm not sure who was more surprised—him or me—but I had just become a Christian, and my life was changing. When the Lord saved me, I was an immoral, rebellious, drug user and dealer. I came to Christ a few days before the end of the fall college term, and it was now the first day of winter term. I had been reading my Bible (a Gideon New Testament handed out on campus) and was beginning to grow in my relationship with the Lord. No one had sat me down and explained that Christians shouldn't take illegal drugs. My choice was based upon something far deeper. The nagging emptiness of life without Christ had been one of the things that drove me to seek the temporary escape of drugs. Suddenly, I discovered that such emptiness was no longer there anymore. God hadn't taken the drugs away; He had taken the desire away. It was never a struggle for me after that. It wasn't that I had tried diligently against that sin and overcame, but rather, that **I had been overcome by Christ,** and He was now living His life through me. I didn't want to walk in darkness anymore now that I had found the light. It is to such living that Paul invites us here in Ephesians chapter 5.

📖 Take a look at Ephesians 5:11. What do you see as the significance of the contrast here.

_____

_____

_____

_____

Not only are we called to not "participate" (literally "have fellowship") in the unfruitful deeds associated with darkness, but we are also called to expose them. The implication is that if we are not exposing the sins of darkness for what they are, we are in essence, giving our approval by our silence. We expose the deeds of darkness by living lives that contradict and define them, and by taking a verbal, biblical stand against them balancing the rightness of God's justice with the truth of His love. Not only do we expose the "wrongness" of the deeds, but we also declare that they are unfruitful. Part of the idea here is that we show a more fruitful life can be found in a relationship with God.

📖 In Ephesians 5:12, Paul again brings up the subject of our speech. How does our speech relate to walking in the light?

_____

_____

_____

_____

This verse gives further clarity to the admonition of 4:29 in defining more specifically one example area of what "unwholesome" speech entails. We are not to vicariously endorse the sinful actions of unbelievers with our speech because these actions are so contrary to the Lord that even to speak of them is a disgrace.

📖 Read through Ephesians 5:13. What are the things spoken of here that become visible when exposed to light?

_____

_____

_____

_____

The _"all things"_ spoken of in this verse that will be exposed by the light obviously points back to the _"unfruitful deeds of darkness"_ spoken of in 5:11. As to the last part (_"everything that becomes visible is light"_), it seems to carry the

Word Study

PARTICIPATING IN FELLOWSHIP

The Greek word translated "participate" here is _sugkoinōnéō_ (from _sun,_ meaning "with," and _koinōnéō_ [to partake, to fellowship with]). It speaks of fellowship. A believer can mingle with unbelievers but will not find the common ground of Christian fellowship among such people.

idea that that which becomes visible is exposed. When we walk in the light, we become light and our lives illumine the darkness around us.

📖 Examine Ephesians 5:14. Why does Paul begin this verse with the phrase, "For this reason. . . ."?

_____

_____

_____

_____

One light in a darkened room changes everything.

The "reason" Paul speaks of here is the truth of the previous verses—that light exposes and manifests the darkness—and may carry with it the idea of light developing light in the exposed darkness either by changed actions or by defining righteousness through the contrast of that which is unrighteous. Remember, darkness cannot put out light. Only light has the power to dispel. One light in a darkened room changes everything.

📖 Verse 14 is a paraphrase of Isaiah 60:1. Read that verse in its context and identify the outcome of the light of Christ shining on us.

_____

_____

_____

_____

Paul's quote from the Old Testament makes an interesting point. As the light of Messiah (Christ) shines on Israel, the result will be that _"nations will come to your light."_ While the context is to Israel, Paul applies the principle to the Ephesian Gentiles. The point he is making is that as Christ's light shines on us, it shines through us, and others will be attracted to Him as a result.

Ephesians 5:1-17
DAY FOUR

WALK LOGICALLY (5:15—17)

What does it mean to "follow"? In the passage where Jesus calls Matthew the tax collecter to _"follow Me"_ (Matthew 9:9), the word "follow" is translated from _akoloutheō_, and a word study of this Greek word paints a beautiful picture for us. The word _akoloutheō_ comes from a root word meaning "road" and conveys the meaning of walking the same path or road. In Jesus' day, people usually walked wherever they needed to go. The students of a Rabbi would often walk with him as he walked about or went on a journey. When Jesus urged others to follow Him, He promised that if they walked with Him they would never walk in darkness (see John 8:12). He would be like a torch or lamp to light the way wherever they went, whenever they went with him. Paul told the Corinthians to _"be imitators of me, just as I also am of Christ"_ (1 Corinthians 11:1). In other words Paul is saying, "I am following Christ. I am walking down the same road with Him. Where He turns, I turn. When He stops, I stop. When He goes, I go. It is a walk in the light because He Himself is "The Light." Now, you imitate me. Follow Christ and walk in the light." If we are truly following Christ, we must let Him lead. Walking wisely requires that we not act "foolish" but _"understand what the will of the Lord is"_ (Ephesians 5:17).

📖 Read through Ephesians 5:15–16 and make a list of the specifics Paul is urging us to do in these verses.

_____

_____

_____

First of all, Paul exhorts us to be careful (literally "look carefully" or "see carefully") how we walk—to take care in how we walk with God. Second, he urges us to not walk as the unwise men, but rather, to walk as the wise do. Finally, he calls us to make the most of (literally "redeem") our time. This phrase *"redeem the time"* is a metaphor akin to traders and merchants who diligently observe and improve the calendar for merchandising and trade.

Look again at verse 16. What is the reason Paul gives for urging us to do that?

_____

_____

_____

Paul urges us to make the most of our time *"because the days are evil."* To make good use of time will require swimming against the tide since Satan rules this world, and unplanned time will tend to flow toward Satan and his purposes. You don't have to intentionally waste time—it happens naturally to those who do not plan otherwise.

📖 Read Ephesians 5:17. How are we supposed to be able to do what Paul urges us to do here?

_____

_____

_____

_____

The only way we will be able to maximize our time use is if we discern God's will day by day through studying the Scriptures (see Psalm 119:105) and through prayer (see James 1:5). God's will is filtered through His omniscience. He never wastes time.

God wants us to walk with Him. He wants us to walk in love, to walk in light, and to walk logically. Most of all, He wants us to trust His lead and follow Him. God has not simply given us a road map for life. He has given Himself as a guide. All we need to do is follow. Will we?

FOR ME TO FOLLOW GOD

Ephesians 5:1–17
DAY FIVE

As we stated in Lesson 8, when one walks about in a dark room there is always a tendency to trip and stumble and bump into unseen objects. But when the lights are turned on, the traveling about is much easier and safer. In the same way, when we walk in God's light, we have purpose, guidance, and direction in life. God didn't create us only to

> "Therefore be careful how you walk, not as unwise men but as wise, making the most of your time, because the days are evil."
>
> Ephesians 5:15–16

> ## "So then do not be foolish, but understand what the will of the Lord is."
>
> ## Ephesians 5:17

leave us to find our own way, but He has given us direction through His Word and guidance through His Spirit. The problem comes when we choose to go our own independent ways. In the same way that we cannot reach God on our own, we cannot live life that God created on our own. The truth of Christianity as God intends it to be, is not just "seeing the light," but having seen the light, to walk in that light. As obedient children, we need to imitate our Father. In order to live life His way we must take time to *"learn what is pleasing to the Lord"* (5:10), and *"understand what the will of the Lord is"* (5:17). Then we can *"walk in the light."*

APPLY The first thing we looked at this week was what it means to walk in love. God wants us to walk in a love relationship with Him, and then express His love to others. According to Scripture, there is a direct link between love and giving. How often do you exhibit a giving heart toward others?

❑ Never

❑ Rarely

❑ Sometimes

❑ Often

❑ Always

How important would you say it is for you to be learning *"what is pleasing to the Lord"* (Ephesians 5:10)?

_____

_____

_____

_____

_____

When you love someone, you want to do what pleases that person. In John 14:15 Jesus said, *"If you love Me, you will keep My commandments."* When we read this verse, we tend to put the emphasis on trying to be obedient to prove we love Christ. In reality, that is the wrong place. It is love of Christ which must come first. If we are not being obedient there is a problem in our relationship. The solution should be to fall more in love with Jesus. Martin Luther said, "Love the Lord and do as you please . . . for if you love the Lord you will do the things which please Him."

APPLY In what ways are you trying to learn what is pleasing to the Lord?

_____

_____

_____

_____

_____

_____

_____

_____

What should you be doing differently to improve in that area? (Think of the things you are learning in Ephesians.)

_____

_____

_____

_____

_____

Psalm 119:105 says, *"Your word is a lamp to my feet and a light to my path."* God's word gives light and direction. The light of God's Word may not show us the end of the path, but like a lantern carried on a journey, it sheds a circle of light showing us the next few steps to take. As we take those steps, "walking in the light," the circle moves and shows us further steps to take. It is difficult to be reflecting the light unless we are receiving the light on a regular basis.

APPLY Do you have time set aside each day to be in the Word of God?

_____

Paul exhorts *"be careful how you walk . . . making the most of your time"* (Ephesians 5:15–16). In order to make the most of our time, we must have a workable plan for managing our time. If you aren't using a time-planning system then you're probably wasting a lot of time. Maybe a good application point to this week's lesson would be to plan a time this week to go out and find a good time-planning system.

It will be worthwhile to put the finishing touches on this lesson by writing out a prayer to the Lord, expressing your heart honestly to Him.

_____

_____

_____

_____

_____

_____

_____

_____

_____

_____

_____

_____

_____

"Your word is a lamp to my feet and a light to my path."

Psalm 119:105

Notes

Ephesians 5:15-21

POWER FOR LIVING

ADVICE FOR THE VICTORIOUS CHRISTIAN WALK

In the book of Acts, the apostle Paul is given two different identities. He is introduced to us at the stoning of Stephen as a young man named Saul. Yet for most of the book of Acts, he is called Paul. The difference is more than cosmetic. Saul, the persecutor of the Church before meeting Christ, is very different than Paul the missionary. Both thought they were following God, yet how differently that following finds its expression. Saul was in *"hearty agreement"* with putting Stephen to death (Acts 8:1). He invested his energies *"ravaging"* the Church, putting both men and women into prison (Acts 8:3). Paul, however, defended the Church and ended his life in prison doing just that (see 2 Timothy 4:6). Saul had a zeal for God, but it was not in accordance with knowledge (see Romans 10:2). He wanted to do the right thing, yet he allowed culture and tradition to define right instead of the Word of God. Paul, on the other hand, followed not tradition, but the risen Christ. His life was no longer directed by ambition or zeal, but by surrender. What has that to do with us? Everything! You see, Saul, before his trip down the Damascus road, was not a believer in the normal sense of the word. He believed everything he knew about God and was zealously trying to follow Him. But he had not yet learned the difference between doing things **for** God and allowing God to do victorious things **through** him. He had to learn how to draw from the right source.

In John 7:38, Jesus tells the people that if they believed in Him, *"From* [their] *innermost being shall flow rivers of living water."*

> **"He who believes in Me, as the Scripture said, 'From his innermost being shall flow rivers of living water.'"**
>
> **John 7:38**

The next verse explains that Jesus was referring to the overflowing life of the Spirit. In Luke 24:49, Jesus tells the disciples to tarry in Jerusalem until they were *"clothed with power from on high."* In Acts 1:8, just before Christ's ascension, He says, *"You shall receive power when the Holy Spirit has come upon you."* In all of these passages the message is clear: *"Apart from Me you can do nothing"* (John 15:5).

WALKING CAREFULLY (5:15—17)

We are called to walk in relationship with God. Such a relationship is what separates Christianity from every other religion. You could effectively reduce every other major world religion into one common denominator. Each offers its particular system as a means for man to try to live the life God desires and requires. Christianity however, doesn't fit this mold. The message of our faith is that we **cannot** live the life God desires and requires through our own efforts. If we could, we wouldn't need a savior. This week we will focus on the apostle Paul's summary of the Christian life—be filled with the Spirit. We will focus on what it means to walk in God's strength instead of our own. Although we began looking at verses 15–17 in the previous lesson, we want to revisit them to set the context for the key verses that will follow.

Reflect on Ephesians 5:15 and think through what the "therefore" in this verse is "there for"?

Make sure your walk exhibits the light in the proper manner

Paul has just explained the significance of our sonship and the necessity of walking consistently. This occurrence of the word "therefore" is yet another signal, marking one of the many "how-tos" of these final three chapters. In this case, the word "therefore" is a precursor to the message of how we are to walk in the light. It will be worthwhile to notice how many times in these final chapters the subject of "walking" comes up.

Why, according to Ephesians 5:16, do we need to "make the most" of our time?

because there are forces out there actively trying to counter what we are doing. If we are lazy or inefficient, we lose that many more opportunities to influence ~~things~~ (people) for Christ

Time, like money, is a perishable commodity. Once it is used it is gone, and all that is left is what it was traded for. Wasted time yields little return on the investment, so "making the most" of our time becomes an issue of being a good steward of what God has entrusted to us. Like money, time is not eternal, but it can be invested in eternal ways through time spent with God and His eternal word, and through energy invested in winning souls.

What do you think the statement in 5:16, *"because the days are evil,"* means?

Sin still dominates much of our culture

> "Therefore be careful how you walk, not as unwise men but as wise...."
>
> **Ephesians 5:15**

Either they are evil because of those who live in them, or evil, full of troubles and dangers by reason of men's antagonism toward Christianity and Christians, which may hinder our opportunities to do good or result in persecution if we do. The world system in power is allied with the evil one, so we should not be surprised that days tend toward evil.

📖 In Ephesians 5:15–17, we are exhorted not to walk unwisely or foolishly. What from the context would characterize one who walks that way?

Coarse joking, drunkenness, greed, impurity covetousness, idolatry,

In looking at the verses that surround these exhortations, several ideas suggest themselves. One who lives life carelessly and without forethought would be walking foolishly. One who doesn't use his time wisely obviously would be unwise. Finally, one who isn't following God's will would be most foolish.

How does the command in Ephesians 5:17 to *"understand what the will of the Lord is"* fit in with this context?

Understanding the will of God, when applied to the context of time-is-short perspective, should prompt us to action in our own lives as well as others

It is impossible to make the most of our time if we are not following God's will, since God created life and through His sovereignty is actively involved with all He created. The wisest possible use of our time will be spent doing God's will. We may not have as much time was we want, but we have enough. God has given each of us enough years, days, hours, and minutes to do all that He has planned for us to do. The question is will we use that time the way He intended, or will we do our own thing with the time He gives us?

WALKING IN THE SPIRIT (5:18)

Ephesians 5:15-21

DAY TWO

Picture in your mind a cold, juicy, luscious bowl of grapes. They are plump and full, with little beads of moisture condensing on their surface. Your mouth waters as you imagine the explosion of flavor as you bite down on one. I don't know about you, but I love grapes. I'm getting hungry just thinking about them! In John 15, Jesus makes an important point about grapes. He says that you and I as believers are like the branches of a grape vine. God wants to produce through us something more attractive and desirable even than those grapes. He wants to produce in us His life. He made us for this very purpose. But for this objective to be realized it takes more than simply being a branch—it takes abiding.

The Bible does not present random and conflicting messages. Instead, it presents the same message multiple ways. Walking in the Spirit, or being "filled" with the Spirit is not something different than abiding in the vine. It is the same message—"stay connected to Christ." The Bible uses other terminology as well. A life of connection with Christ is also called "walking in the light," or being *"crucified with Christ"* (Galatians 2:20), or "walking by faith." It all boils down to this—we must allow God to be in control of our lives.

📖 What do you see as the significance of linking Ephesians 5:17–18 with the word "and"?

That our promptness and light-bearing should be under
the control and direction of the Spirit and not of our
own design.

The obvious implication is that being *"filled with the Spirit"* is an essential component of the *"will of the Lord"* and of *"making the most of your time."* Although verse 18 is usually quoted by itself, the connective "and" binds it to the preceding verses and indicates that all verses in context should bear directly on the interpretation of verse 18.

What do you see in the context of Ephesians 5:18 that relates to the command not to get drunk with wine?

Control - or giving it up, rather, to God or wine.

When one partakes of alcohol in excess, the person begins to lose control and the alcohol begins to control that person's actions. The person can no longer think or act clearly, so obviously it would be impossible for that person to make the most of his or her time. You can say that one who impairs his or her mental capacities through consuming too much alcohol is one who is foolish.

Continue to think about this idea of being *"drunk with wine"* (5:18). In what ways would this be similar to being filled with the Spirit?

Wine reduces your capacity to make decisions and control
yourself appropriately

Volunteering your control to the Spirit willingly reduces
your capacity to do the same on your own.

"And do not get drunk with wine, for that is dissipation, but be filled with the Spirit...."

Ephesians 5:18

A person who is drunk with wine experiences altered behavior. Such a person becomes under the influence of alcohol and thinks and acts differently than he or she would without it. So too it is with one who is under the influence of the Spirit of God. While the altered behavior of one who is drunk usually results in negative behavior, the opposite is true of one filled with the Spirit.

What do you think it means to be "filled" with the Spirit (5:18)?

Giving the Spirit such sway in your life as to listen to no other direction or influence. Including your own sinful desires

The Greek verb form "to be filled" (*pleróō*) used in this case doesn't mean to get more of the Spirit since the Spirit indwells us completely when we are born spiritually. It is not an issue of us getting more of the Spirit, but rather, of the Spirit getting more of us. It has the idea of being directed (see Luke 4:1) and empowered (see Acts 10:38) by God's Spirit. Although the Holy Spirit is always resident in our lives, He is not always allowed to be in charge. It is the "filling" that makes Him so. This verse literally reads "be filled by the Spirit" which makes perfect sense in this context.

One might speak of the filling of the Spirit in this manner: while He is resident in the life of every true Christian, He is not always president. The Spirit may be living in the heart, but He is not always allowed to control and direct that heart. He will not force Himself on us, but when we are willing to yield, He takes charge and the result is always for the better.

Word Study
DISSIPATION

The Greek word translated "dissipation," *asōtía* (from *a* [negative prefix], and *sṓzō*, meaning "to save," giving the idea of waste that is irretrievable), has the same root word as is used in Luke 15:13 ("loose living") of the prodigal son. It carries the idea of a debauched, lascivious, or profligate manner of living, wasteful excess, or one who extravagantly squanders his means.

WALKING IN THE SPIRIT (CONTINUED)

Ephesians 5:15-21
DAY THREE

People notice a difference when someone is drunk. They see distinct changes in manner such as a staggering walk or a slurring of speech. They witness altered behavior—seeing the intoxicated one become more boisterous and exuberant. It isn't hard to tell when someone has been drinking. Is it difficult for others to tell who has been drinking of the living waters? It shouldn't be. There ought to be a noticeable difference in our lives from God's Spirit being in control. Of course, the behavior of one under the influence of the Holy Spirit is not a negative one as it would be with one under the influence of alcohol. People under the influence of the Spirit of God manifest the fruit of that Spirit: *"love, joy, peace, patience, kindness, goodness, faithfulness, gentleness, self-control"* (Galatians 5:22–23). What a positive change occurs in us when God is in charge of our lives!

Compare Ephesians 5:18 with Acts 2:4 and 4:31 and ask yourself, *Is this a once for all act or can it be repeated?*

Seems to be a temporary condition of interaction of the spirit working through men.

Ephesians 5:15-21

These verses, as well as others in the book of Acts that are directed toward the same group of people, indicate that the filling of the Spirit is an act that can be repeated. As we disobey and take control of our lives, there is a need to yield control back to the Spirit of God indwelling us.

How do you see being filled with the Spirit as different from being "sealed" with the Spirit (Ephesians 1:13–14; 4:30)?

The seal is a mark of ownership. that doesn't change as we drift to and from being full of the spirit.

Being "sealed" with the Spirit is a once and for all experience that occurs at salvation and is concurrent with being "baptized" by the Spirit into Christ's family (see 1 Corinthians 12:13). Being "filled with the Spirit" is a repeatable act that is part of the sanctification process. Being "sealed" with the Spirit deals with you getting the Spirit; whereas, being "filled with the Spirit" involves the Spirit getting you.

In Ephesians 5:18, the verb form *"be filled"* is in the imperative mood. It is a command, not a suggestion. Why is it significant that we are **commanded** to be filled with the Spirit?

It is an integral part of the Christian walk. It isn't just the "higher level" that is achieved by "super-christians" + a reward for those who are duly faithful. Rather, it's an expectation for ALL who want to walk with the LORD.

Being filled with the Spirit is not an optional accessory to the Christian life. It is the hub of walking consistently with God. There is no other way to experience the victorious Christian life except for the indwelling Christ to be in control (see John 15:5). To not be "filled" (directed and empowered) with the Spirit is to disobey a direct command of Scripture and is therefore sin.

There is no place in Scripture that indicates we can receive more of the Holy Spirit, nor is there any indication since the advent of the Spirit at Pentecost (see Acts 2) that He ever leaves us. The real issue is the release of the already present Spirit to have free reign in our hearts. It isn't about us getting more of Him, but of Him getting more of us.

WALKING IN THE BODY (5:19—21)

No person is an island. No one can go through life without interacting with others. God created us as relational beings. Yet sadly, many of our relationships are fractured and stained by sin. Of course, all relationships begin with our relationship to God. The dynamic of that supernatural relationship holds great sway over the quality of all our earthly relationships. If all is not well in our relationship with God, our relationships with others will be negatively affected. But the flip side of that coin is true as well. If we are filled with the Spirit of God—if He is on the throne of our hearts and in control of our lives—then all our human relationships will be positively affected. We will be a blessing to all who cross our paths. We will encourage them with the refreshing presence of God which will be real in us. Instead of looking to our relationships for what we can take from others, we will begin to see relationships in light of what we can give. Finding our own deepest needs met in our relationship with God, we will be free to be used by Him to meet needs in others. What a wonderful world this would be if everyone were Spirit-filled!

📖 How, according to Ephesians 5:19, will being Spirit-filled affect our relationships with others?

our relationships should be conducted as to the Lord.

If Christ is on the throne of our hearts, all our human relationships will be affected in a positive way. We'll be speaking in healthy ways, instead of in the wrong speech patterns dealt with in previous passages we have studied. If we are Spirit-filled, we will be speaking to one another. We'll have something to say and the freedom to say it. Such acts of freedom probably include both speaking in the literal sense of teaching, as well as speaking casually in regular interaction with other believers. The content of our conversing with others will be both edifying and glorifying to God.

Reread Ephesians 5:19, focusing on the last half of the verse. How will being Spirit-filled affect our relationship with God?

our hearts (inner desires & thoughts) will be as a melody to God, or something pleasing to Him

When we are "Spirit-filled," we will be singing. Obviously the practice of singing is featured prominently in most church worship services. One result of singing is that when we are participating in the corporate singing spoken of in this verse, we do it not just with our voices but with our hearts as well. Another, less obvious meaning, would seem to suggest that Spirit-filled believers have a song in their hearts—an inner joy. Both meanings or interpretations of this verse are probably implied. Singing plays an important role in our worship of God. Our singing does not serve each other or serve as a time filler, but it is offered *"to the Lord,"* and it flows from a full heart. It is impossible to truly worship God apart from being Spirit-filled (see John 4:24).

📖 Take a look at Ephesians 5:20. How does *"always giving thanks for all things"* fit in with the Spirit-filled life?

recognizing that all things are from the Lord, even the difficult ones, makes a Spirit-filled life possible

Did You Know?

PSALMS, HYMNS, AND SPIRITUAL SONGS

The particular distinction of "psalms" as well as "hymns" and "spiritual songs" is uncertain, but most view them this way:

PSALMS: the book of this name basically represented the Jewish hymnbook and consisted of the ancient songs sung to musical accompaniment.

HYMNS: limited to songs of praise.

SPIRITUAL SONGS: general Christian songs that were doctrinal, prophetic, or historical but not part of Scripture.

The implication of this phrase, *"always giving thanks for all things"* is that one of the evidences of being "filled" with the Spirit involves sharing a consistent attitude of thankfulness. Paul says we do this *"always"*—as a matter of habit, throughout the course of our life. He also says we give thanks *"for all things"*—not just for life's pleasantries or for positional blessings but for our trials and afflictions as well, since we trust that God uses even these in the sanctification process (see Romans 8:28).

Look at Ephesians 5:20 again. What do you think it means that giving thanks is to be done *"in the name of our Lord Jesus Christ"*?

> Jesus name is what unlocks the Spirit to inhabit us at all. Through His sacrifice, we have access in the first place.

"In Jesus' name" is much more than just a biblical way to say "the end" as we finish a prayer. It is because of the work of Christ that we can pray confidently. Hebrews 10:19 tells us that we can enter the "Holy Place" (the presence of God) with confidence by the shed blood of Jesus. To pray "in Jesus' name" is to verbally affirm the work of Christ in establishing communication and communion with God. It also means that we are coming to God in His righteousness, not in our own. If we were holy apart from Christ, we could pray in our own names.

📖 Read Ephesians 5:21. What does it mean to be "subject" to one another?

> Willing to accept admonishment as well as giving it in love.

To be *"subject"* to one another carries the idea of mutual submission to our brethren in Christ out of love. It involves bearing one another's burdens, and rejoicing with one another's victories as opposed to self-promotion and advancement. It also involves humbly fulfilling our God-given role with a servant's heart rather than "lording" our leadership over others as unbelievers do (see Matthew 20:25–28).

Look at Ephesians 5:21 again. Why is this being subject to one another done in the *"fear of Christ"*?

> So that no one views their admonishing another christian as a position higher than they should, even though another has submitted themselves to us, we still must remain submitted to Christ

"Fear of Christ," as with fear of God, doesn't involve fear of what God may do to us or how He may treat us, but rather, has the idea of viewing Him with a healthy reverence and respect. The context, as well as biblical usage, links this phrase with placing ourselves under His leadership and submitting to Him as a child would to a parent.

When we are under the influence of the Spirit of God, we are different people than those who do not know God or those who do not walk in fellowship with Him. We build healthy relationships with others instead of isolating ourselves from people. While under the influence of the Holy Spirit, we have a song in our hearts, and when we sing, our singing is offered to the Lord. Our attitudes are pervaded by thankfulness. Most importantly, when we are Spirit-filled, we are "subject" to one another. Submission is not hard for one who is Spirit-filled. But it is impossible for those who are not. We need the empowering work of the Spirit to live the abundant life Christ promised.

FOR ME TO FOLLOW GOD

The Christian life, that is, living life as God intends, is a life of purpose and power. In Chapter 1, Paul prays that the "eyes of our heart" would grasp the power of God that is ours because we are His. We experience this "power for living" when we are "filled" (directed and empowered) by the Spirit of God. The problem is that our lives, much like a car, have only one driver's seat. If we insist on directing our own lives, then God graciously steps aside—but fortunately He never leaves us (see Hebrews 13:5). He is still "resident" in our lives but no longer "president" because He will not force Himself on us. The result is that, although we still possess the blessings of God (our riches, hope, and power [Ephesians 1:18–19]), we no longer experience them. In the same way that salvation is God's work not man's, the Christian life is God's responsibility. To experience it we must, as Paul exhorts, *be filled with the Spirit.*

Who is in the driver's seat of your life?

 APPLY The real issue of this week's lesson is "who is in the driver's seat of your life?"

Circle where you spend the most time:

Spirit–filled ←———— 1 ———— 2 ———— ③ ← ④ ———— 5 ————→ self–directed

Christians who characteristically lead a self-directed life do so for one of two reasons—lack of knowledge or lack of belief. They are either uninformed of or have forgotten the abundant life Christ promises. Which deficiency is more relevant to your experience and the times when you are not close to the Lord?

Forgotten.

Ask yourself this question: "Do I honestly want God to direct my life?" If the answer is "Yes," then go on; if the answer is "No," then talk honestly with God about this and ask Him to change your heart. God knows our hearts. It is useless to talk spiritually with religious-sounding terminology if our hearts are not sincere. If you really don't want God to direct your life, tell Him that, and invite Him to help you deal with that attitude. Often wrong attitudes never change because we never bring them to the One who can change them (and change us as well).

_____

_____

_____

_____

_____

_____

In chapter 4, Paul relates the two principles of being filled with the Spirit, and he uses the figurative language of changing clothes—laying aside the old self and putting on the new self. The following explains how we do that.

Laying Aside the Old Self

First, you must confess the general sin of directing your own life. If you have been wearing the old garments of self, then the real problem is not the specific "sins" that creep up, but the general sin of self being in control.

Next, ask God to reveal any specific sins He wants to deal with and confess them using 1 John 1:9 as a promise. Once we have dealt with the general sin of running our own life, there will probably be specific individual sins that will also need to be addressed.

It is crucial that we understand what it means to "confess." The Greek word for "confess" means "to say the same thing" or "to agree." When we confess our sins, we are agreeing to three things. First, we agree that the action or attitude is wrong. We agree with God's perspective on it. Second, we agree that we are guilty and need to change. Third, we agree that our sin is forgiven. We choose to see it as Christ does.

We cannot wear the new garment without taking off the old. We must put self aside. But taking off the old garment is not enough. We must also "put on" the new. How do we do this?

Putting on the New Self

The first step to putting on the new garment is to invite Christ to take control of the throne of your life and ask God to fill you with His Holy Spirit as He commands you to be. In a word, this step is to "yield."

Second, we must thank Him by faith for filling us with His Spirit. We know that it is His will for us to be Spirit-filled because He commands it. We know according to the promise in 1 John 5:14–15 that when we pray according to His will, He hears us and answers us.

We do not judge whether or not God has filled us with His Spirit by our feelings. We may or may not have an emotional experience. We must walk by faith, not by feelings, and we must trust God to do what He promised.

Doctrine
CONFESSION

When we confess sin, we are agreeing with God about that sin. We are choosing to see it as He does. We look at what He calls sin, and we call it sin. We call ourselves guilty and must be willing to repent. And most importantly, we call ourselves forgiven, for that is God's perspective that we must also agree with.

Why not close out this week's lesson by expressing your faith in God's working in the form of a written prayer to Him?

_____

_____

_____

_____

_____

_____

_____

_____

_____

_____

_____

_____

_____

_____

_____

_____

_____

_____

_____

Notes

Ephesians 5:21—6:9

THE MISSION OF SUBMISSION
GOD'S DESIGN FOR OUR FAMILIES AND OUR CAREERS

Have you heard the story about the young man who was sick and tired of his parents telling him what to do? He wanted to be out on his own without his dad's restrictions and rules—so he ran away from home and joined the Marines! Boy, was he in for a rude awakening! Much as we may wish it were otherwise, submission to the authorities God places over us is something we will never outgrow. Everyone answers to someone. While we may outgrow our parents' authority, we will never outgrow the principle of authorities in our lives. We will have bosses and supervisors or we may report to clients and boards. We answer to policemen and political leaders. We submit to the tax laws and speed limits. (Or, if we don't, we are reminded of why we should.) We may have landlords and civic authorities as well as spiritual leaders such as pastors and elders. Submission is not something we will ever outgrow. Even if we are the king and absolute ruler of a country, we still must submit to authority. Just ask Nebuchadnezzar.

Nebuchadnezzar was king of Babylon at the time of the prophet Daniel. King Nebuchadnezzar boasted in Daniel 4:30, "Is this not Babylon the great, which I myself have built as a royal residence by the might of my power and for the glory of my majesty?" He thought he was the ultimate authority and answered to no one. But while the words were still on his lips, his kingdom was taken away, and he became a lunatic, eating grass like a cow for seven years. It was not until he lifted his

Submission is not something we will ever outgrow.

head toward heaven to acknowledge God that his kingdom and his reason were restored. He had to learn the hard way that everyone has to submit to someone sometime. And he eventually did learn from his mistaken pride. His testimony in Daniel 4:37 is this: *"Now I, Nebuchadnezzar, praise, exalt and honor the King of heaven, for all His works are true and His ways just, and He is able to humble those who walk in pride."*

God has placed authorities and leaders in everyone's life. We are responsible before Him to submit to them, and there is a reason for this. What is the real mission of this submission? God uses human authorities and leaders to teach us how to submit to Him as our ultimate authority. This is the mission of submission.

Ephesians
5:21—6:9

DAY ONE

HUSBANDS AND WIVES (5:21—33)

In Ephesians chapters 5 and 6, Paul lists four different areas of submission: believers to one another (5:21), wives to husbands (5:22–33), children to parents (6:1–4), and slaves to masters (6:5–9). In each case, Paul makes it clear that this submission is not a one-way street. He reveals in this passage that there are divine responsibilities on "both sides of the fence." While often much is made of the role of the follower to submit, we must remain true to the text. There are also great responsibilities for the leaders as well, for they too are to be followers of God and in submission to His headship. This is God's plan. Today we will begin looking forward to what this passage teaches about the roles of husbands and wives. But before we do this, we need to look back to a statement in last week's lesson which frames the context of Paul's admonition to husbands and wives and which balances out the submitting called for in the verses that follow.

📖 Read Ephesians 5:21. How does this verse in the context of the Spirit-filled life, fit in with the verses that follow regarding submission?

_____

_____

_____

_____

Word Study
SUBMISSION

The Greek word translated "be subject" (*hupotásso*) means "to line one's self up under, to submit." It was used in a military sense of soldiers submitting to their superiors or slaves submitting to their masters. The word primarily has the idea of giving up one's own right or will. It is this truth of mutual submission that keeps any God-given authority from running over a child of God.

Verse 21 begins with the word "and" indicating a tight link with the preceding passage, yet its content points to what follows. The obvious implication is that there is a direct relationship between submission and being Spirit-filled. If we are Spirit-filled, we will submit ourselves to all authority. Conversely, true submission from the heart is an impossibility apart from the Spirit's empowering. It is also important to recognize that there is a mutual submission between believers apart from the line of authority.

📖 What do you see as the significance of the qualifying statement in verse 22, *"as to the Lord"*?

_____

_____

_____

As Paul says wives are to be subject to their husbands *"as to the Lord,"* he may be implying that wives are to be in compliance with God's authority over them since God commands them to submit to their husbands. Another idea that Paul may have had in mind is that women who submit to their husbands do so in the same way they would to God—in a like manner of honor and respect. Regardless of what Paul had in mind, both possibilities are in line with scriptural teaching. A wife is not being submissive to God's leading if she is not being submissive to her husband.

📖 Take a look at Ephesians 5:23. What insights can be drawn from the correlation between husbands and wives and Christ and the Church?

_____

_____

_____

_____

The most obvious correlation between these two is that as Christ is the head of the church, the husband is to be the head of the wife. This is an open/shut case with no room for argument. If you devalue the role of the husband as leader and authority, you are saying the same thing about Christ's role in the Church, since the husband is to be an earthly picture of the heavenly reality. Another aspect that is implied is that it is to be a relationship where the husband loves and serves his wife in leading and taking responsibility for her. What prevents the act of submitting to the husband from becoming an act of devaluing the wife is the fact that leading is about serving in the kingdom of God. To be the head of the home is not a position of greater privilege but rather a position of greater responsibility.

📖 Read through Ephesians 5:25. How does loving fit in with giving yourself up?

_____

_____

_____

_____

The husband is to exhibit Christ's love to his wife in every way, and the highest demonstration of Christ's love was through giving Himself as a sacrifice for our sins. Likewise, the husband is called to give himself sacrificially for his wife. This sacrificial giving does not just involve physical sacrifice, but more importantly, it involves a regular laying aside of his rights and needs until first insuring that those of his wife are met. A woman should have little difficulty submitting to a sacrificial leader.

📖 Identify Christ's objectives for His Church in verses 26 and 27 and relate them to the husband.

_____

_____

_____

_____

The bottom line of submission on every level is not "Can I trust this leader," but "Can I trust God to work in, through, and in spite of this leader?"

Like Christ's objectives for His church, the husband should have as his aim for his wife **a)** her sanctification; **b)** a renewed mind from the Word; **c)** her glorification and presentation to Christ; and **d)** her spiritual growth toward becoming holy and blameless in her experience and not just in her position.

God has a plan and an order for life, and this plan includes submission. Everyone must live by this life principle, and faith is at submission's core. When I submit to the leaders God places over me, I do so not in trust of them, but in trust of God who placed them. My trust is not that they will always make the right decisions, but rather, that God is able to work in their hearts and in my life even in their mistakes. The bottom line of submission on every level is not "Can I trust this leader," but "Can I trust God to work in, through, and in spite of this leader?"

Ephesians
5:21—6:9

DAY TWO

HUSBANDS AND WIVES (CONTINUED)

In this age of emphasis on feminism and equal rights for all, many stumble over the Christian concept of the husband being the head of the home. Perhaps it is difficult for many to accept this concept because of the failure of many Christian husbands to lead as Christ did. Jesus said that Gentile (or unbelieving) leadership usually resulted in their "lording" it over those they led. In Matthew 20:26 Jesus responded, *"It is not this way among you, but whoever wishes to become great among you shall be your servant."* Being the head of the home does not mean that the husband is worth more than the wife. What it means is that God has appointed someone to serve by leading. This does not give the husband a "better deal" or more freedom. Instead, it gives him greater responsibility and greater accountability to the One to whom he reports—the Lord.

📖 Read through Ephesians 5:26 and determine its immediate context. What do you think it meant to be cleansed by the *"washing of water with the word"*?

_____

_____

_____

_____

_____

_____

_____

Word Study
THE WORD

There are two main Greek terms translated "word," each with subtly different meanings. The term *"logos"* (from which we get our English word "logic") places the emphasis on the content itself. The term *"rhēma"* (from which we get our English word "rhetoric") comes from a noun which means "to speak." It emphasizes not only the message but the communication of the message. *Rhēma* is the word translated "word" in Ephesians 5:26.

Some have suggested that this phrase, *"the washing of water with the word,"* points to the sacrament of baptism and the "word" as being that of the gospel message. This doesn't seem consistent with the practical exhortations of the context, however. More likely, the verse is analogous of bathing, implying that just as water cleanses the body physically, the Word of God cleanses the body spiritually—especially the mind which must be renewed (see Romans 12:1–2). This passage indicates that it is the husband's responsibility to ground his wife in the Word of God.

144 FOLLOWING GOD – THE BOOK OF EPHESIANS

📖 Take a look at Ephesians 5:28–29. Why are husbands to consider wives as their own bodies and flesh?

_____

_____

_____

_____

There are three main reasons why a husband should see his wife as his own flesh. First, and most obvious, a husband should view his wife in this way because it is a command of God (verse 33). Second, it is in the husband's best interests to do so, since she is a part of him and is his "help meet" (Genesis 2:18 KJV). Finally, it is all important for the husband to love his wife in this way because his relationship with his wife is to be an earthly portrait of Christ's love for, commitment to, and identification with His church.

📖 Evaluate the statement made in Ephesians 5:30. How does it relate to the husband?

_____

_____

_____

_____

Because Christ has identified with us and we identify with Him, we are a part of Him now (1:23). In the same way, the husband is to consider his wife as a part of himself. This concept of one body points all the way back to Eve, who was made from Adam's body (his rib [Genesis 2:21–22]). A husband who does not care for his wife as part of himself is in fact, hurting himself.

📖 Read over Ephesians 5:31–32 and answer the questions that follow.

What is the significance of the husband and wife cleaving and becoming "one flesh"?

_____

_____

_____

_____

How does this concept relate to Christ and the Church?

_____

_____

_____

_____

Paul starts out verses 31 and 32 with the statement, "for this reason." The "reason" he refers to would seem to be the goal of oneness. It also most likely has in view Eve's creation out of Adam since this is the original context of the Old Testament quote found in verse 31 (see Genesis 2:24). The point is this: since woman has her origin in man, it is God's intent that through marriage she returns to that bond in a permanent way. This serves as an excellent picture of the believer's relationship to Christ. The believer has his origin in Christ since Christ created all things (see Colossians 1:16), and through salvation he is restored to that relationship in a permanent way.

📖 Looking at Ephesians 5:33, why do you think the husband is exhorted to *"love his own wife"* while the wife is exhorted to see to it that she *"respects her husband"*?

_____

_____

_____

_____

_____

Certainly the wife is to love her husband and the husband is to respect his wife. The reason Paul singles out the particular exhortations is probably because of weaknesses unique to each. The husband will be more likely to struggle with loving than respecting, because society grooms him toward respect. The wife on the other hand will more likely have little trouble loving her husband because of her more emotive bent, but she will struggle with giving her husband the respect he deserves. This is also an indication that perhaps the husband has a greater need for respect while the wife has more need for love.

Much is made of the responsibility of the wife to submit herself to the husband, but often not enough is made of the husband's responsibilities. He is to lead her. He is to love her and give up himself for her like Jesus did for us. He is to pursue her sanctification and renewed mind according to the Word. He is to seek to present her holy and blameless. He is to nourish and cherish her. All of these qualities seem to be a practical outworking of the mutual subjection that Ephesians 5:21 speaks to all of us. Just because the husband is the leader doesn't mean he isn't to be subject.

This section of Ephesians is very rich and practical. It offers a blueprint for the husband and wife relationship. But we must not miss the fact that something larger than this is also in view. Paul is showing God's plan for how the Church is to relate to Christ. One of the reasons Satan attacks the family is because he wants to distort this important teaching tool. He loves divorce because it sends an incorrect message about Christ and the Church.

PARENTS AND CHILDREN (6:1—4)

The mission of submission is expressed in the husband and wife relationship. Although most of us will eventually marry, there is another place where submission must be learned that is relevant to all of us. Not all of us have husbands or wives, but we all have been given biological parents. Hopefully, we get to enjoy this significant relationship and training ground for godly living until we reach adulthood. However, we

> *"Nevertheless, each individual among you also is to love his own wife even as himself, and the wife must see to it that she respects her husband."*
>
> *Ephesians 5:33*

Ephesians 5:21—6:9

DAY THREE

know that Satan loves to target homes and delights when they are fractured by sin and selfishness. But when the family works right, it is the most significant unit of any culture. The state of the family has a direct impact on the state of the country and culture in which we live. Again, we will see that both parents and children have responsibilities as both keep themselves in subjection to Christ.

📖 Looking at Ephesians 6:1, what do you think the exhortation means to obey your parents "*in the Lord*"?

_____

_____

_____

Some view the qualifying statement "*in the Lord*" that follows the command to obey your parents as a limitation to the command. According to this interpretation, we are to obey our parents so long as it doesn't conflict with our duty to God. More likely however, it has in mind the same principle as in 5:22—being subject "*as to the Lord.*" There is no human authority that has not been ordained by God (Romans 13:1), and He is able to work in even a non-Christian parent or leader's heart to accomplish His purposes (see Exodus 10:1; Proverbs 21:1).

📖 Read Ephesians 6:1–2 and answer the questions below.

What do you think is the difference between honoring and obeying?

_____

_____

_____

_____

Which do you think is harder to do?

_____

_____

_____

To honor (*timáō*) our parents means "to value or esteem" whereas to obey them (*hupakoúō*) means to "hearken, to submit and obey." Honoring is an attitude, and obeying is an action. Honoring would seem to be the harder of the two to do, since we can obey even if our attitudes are bad, but to have an attitude of honoring requires that all is right on the inside.

📖 Look up the quote in Ephesians 6:2–3 in its Old Testament context (Exodus 20:12; Deuteronomy 5:16). How would honoring your mother and father result in the effect spoken of in verse 3?

_____

_____

_____

_____

_____

> **"Children, obey your parents in the Lord, for this is right. HONOR YOUR FATHER AND MOTHER (which is the first commandment with a promise). . . ."**
>
> **Ephesians 6:1–2**

In the cases of both Old Testament passages, the specific promise is living long in the Promised Land. To the believer, Canaan represents dwelling in the will of God and the abundant life that results. By honoring our parents we experience this blessing since this is one of God's Ten Commandments to which we are accountable. Another reason we are blessed by honoring our parents is because it is the duty of parents to teach the will and ways of God to their children. Hopefully our obedience to our parents places us in God's will.

📖 Read Ephesians 6:4. In what ways could a father provoke his children to anger?

_____

_____

_____

_____

> ## "Fathers, do not provoke your children to anger, but bring them up in the discipline and instruction of the Lord."
>
> ### Ephesians 6:4

Certainly children can and do become angry without provocation. Sometimes they become angry because of rebellion against godly parental accountablity. This verse is not advocating a parental policy of appeasement—doing anything and everything to pacify children in an effort to keep them from ever becoming angry. What the verse is saying is that our parenting should not be conducted in such a way that it becomes the root cause of our children's anger. In a nutshell, fathers can *"provoke"* children to anger whenever their leadership deviates from *"the discipline and instruction of the Lord."* We get this idea from the contrasting word, *"but."* Anger-provoking parenting may be by discipline that is unjust, inconsistent, or that is not preceded by the proper instruction. We can also provoke our children to anger when the right thing is not done from a right heart of love.

Looking at Ephesians 6:4, why do you think the father bears the responsibility of bringing up the children in *"the discipline and instruction of the Lord"*?

_____

_____

_____

_____

_____

The obvious reason is because God has ordained it that way. One main reason God desires this is because the way the child views his heavenly Father is shaped in part by the actions and leadership of his earthly father. A child's perception is also a logical outworking of God, placing the husband/father as the "head" of the home as a picture of Christ's relationship to the Church. One place where this concept of the "Fatherhood" of God can be clearly seen is in Jesus' parable of the prodigal son (see Luke 15:11–32).

It should be noted that this admonition does not mean that the father alone bears this responsibility. He is the leader of a team which is accountable to this task of bringing the children up in the discipline and instruction of the Lord. The wife must also play a role, as should the extended family and the local church. It is the father's role to give leadership to this process.

SLAVES AND MASTERS (6:5—9)

At a glance, it might appear that this last section of the passage dealing with submission is the least relevant. Since slavery is illegal and not practiced in most developed countries, what could biblical instruction on slavery have to say to us? It is important when we look at Scripture that we look not only at the plans and programs addressed there, but also at the principles behind them. While most of us aren't slaves, there are still principles in the relationship between slaves and masters that relate directly to us today. In the culture of Bible times, most everyone was either self-employed or a slave or servant. In other words, a lot of people back then had bosses.

📖 Read over Ephesians 6:5. How does the phrase *"in the sincerity of your heart, as to Christ"* affect this verse?

_____

_____

_____

_____

Did You Know?
SLAVERY

Slavery in the culture of Israel was very different than slavery in pre-Civil War America. Often in Israel, people became slaves because of debts they had incurred. The Law guaranteed these slaves certain rights. Since most all non-slaves were in business for themselves, slaves were much like the "employees" of today, working for a boss who shares in the benefit of their labor.

The word for sincerity used here literally means "singleness." The implication is of single-mindeness to follow Christ through submission to the earthly master. Since all human authority is *"a minister of God"* (Romans 13:4), then any act of submission to human authority is submission to Christ, and likewise any rebellion. Paul is calling us to see things as they really are in this area of submission. It should be noted that the teaching on slaves and masters applies equally well to the employer/employee relationships in our society since in Paul's day you were either in business for yourself or were a servant (slave).

📖 Look at Ephesians 6:6.

What do you think the terms *"eyeservice"* and *"men-pleasers"* mean?

_____

_____

_____

_____

Can you list some illustrations of these two terms based on your definition of them?

_____

_____

_____

_____

_____

"Eyeservice" has the idea of serving faithfully only when someone is watching or the results will be seen. A "men-pleaser" is one who is concerned only with pleasing men (specifically the master), or more concerned with that

than with pleasing God. Most of us should have no trouble coming up with examples of this practice in others as well as in ourselves.

Look at verse 6 again. How does being a "slave of Christ" fit in with this?

_____

_____

_____

_____

_____

A "slave (*doulos*) of Christ" is a phrase drawing on the cultural picture of a bondservant (see Exodus 21:5–6; Deuteronomy 15:12–18), one who was by choice a servant for life. A bondservant was one who made this lifelong choice out of a motivation of love for his master and recognition that life was better in his service. The picture of a bondservant is a beautiful illustration of what motivates the believer to obedience and service to God. Since we are called to be love-slaves (*doulos*) of Christ, we are responsible to make sure that all we do is pleasing to Him.

Examine verse 6 one more time and answer the questions that follow.

What is the will of God in the situation spoken of in this verse?

_____

_____

_____

_____

What does it mean to do God's will *"from the heart"*?

_____

_____

_____

The "will of God" (verse 6) in this situation is our obedience to our earthly masters, and we are called to do that *"from the heart."* In other words, we are to be obedient to our masters not just in outward obedience, but with an inner (heart) attitude of submission and respect. This obedience with a proper attitude is much harder than mere external obeying.

📖 Look over Ephesians 6:7. How would rendering service *"as to the Lord, and not to men"* affect our attitude?

_____

_____

_____

_____

Certainly not all earthly masters adequately compensate, care for, and appreciate their servants, but even in the most negative situations (or should I say, especially then) we can maintain a good attitude if we focus on being

"With good will render service, as to the Lord, and not to men...."

Ephesians 6:7

pleasing to God in how we serve our masters. This makes our service much easier and more pleasant.

📖 Now read Ephesians 6:8. How should the truth in verse 8 impact this rendering of service "*as to the Lord*?"

_____

_____

_____

_____

It should motivate us to realize that God will reward our actions accordingly both in this life and in the one to come. We see all we do as well as the motive of the heart when we do it (see 1 Corinthians 4:5). As Paul points out in Galatians 6:7, "*do not be deceived, God is not mocked; for whatever a man sows, this he will also reap.*"

📖 How, according to Ephesians 6:9, does this principle of God rewarding apply to the master?

_____

_____

_____

_____

It should be noted that the phrase in verse 5, "*. . . according to the flesh*" makes it clear that this refers to earthly masters, and here it is clarified further as Paul points out the fact that the earthly master is just as accountable to please God with his attitudes and actions as the slave. God is not partial to the master.

The slave and master relationship seems to be a relic of the past. Yet as we have seen today, the principle applies very directly to the relationship of an employee and his boss. Isn't it amazing how practical and timeless the truths of God's Word are!

FOR ME TO FOLLOW GOD

Most of us at some point or another have problems submitting, yet we all have to submit nonetheless. The problems come from not being able to see beyond the immediate situation. The real "mission of submission" is to teach us a higher truth—that of rightly relating to God. In each example Paul gives in Ephesians 5 and 6, our focus is drawn back to this. In 1 John 4:20, John points out that there is a direct correlation between how we relate to others and how we relate to God. Human authority is a "*minister of God*" (Romans 13:4) to develop us in our ability to be good followers. Conversely, "*He who resists authority has opposed the ordinance of God*" (13:2). Therefore, we must choose to let submission accomplish its mission in our lives. The following questions are meant to be an aid in that process.

"**Do not be deceived, God is not mocked; for whatever a man sows, this he will also reap.**"

Galatians 6:7

Ephesians 5:21—6:9

DAY FIVE

"**The real 'mission of submission' is to teach us a higher truth—that of rightly relating to God.**"

APPLY What are some of the particular kinds of authority toward which you have had trouble submitting?

_____

_____

_____

_____

_____

Have you ever viewed them as "ministers of God"?

_____

_____

_____

_____

Identify some of the trouble spots for you right now in the area of submission.

_____ parents	_____ government
_____ traffic laws	_____ school rules
_____ employer	_____ God
_____ other _____	

What do you plan to do differently as a result of this lesson?

_____

_____

_____

_____

The context of this passage seems to indicate that the only way to submit *"in the sincerity of your heart, as to Christ"* (Ephesians 6:5) is through allowing yourself to be directed and empowered by God's Holy Spirit. Review the previous lesson (Lesson 10) and view it with this in mind.

Why not close out this lesson with a written prayer to the Lord?

_____

_____

_____

_____

_____

_____

_____

_____

_____

Notes

Notes

Ephesians 6:10-24

ONWARD CHRISTIAN SOLDIERS
HOW TO BE STRONG IN THE MIDST OF SPIRITUAL WARFARE

One of the most popular topics of discussion in the body of Christ today is the subject called "spiritual warfare." The prominence this subject is afforded is not surprising, and I believe it will become more and more relevant in the days ahead. As you read the Gospel accounts, it doesn't take long to see that there seemed to be much more overt demonic activity in Palestine at the time of Christ than there is in America today. But that is not true of our world as a whole, and even in the Western world that is changing. Western culture is moving away from secular humanism and more toward what some have called a "cosmic humanism," a man-centered belief system with the added dimension of the supernatural. This is reflected in the rapid embracing and repackaging of Eastern mystic beliefs into what is called the New Age movement. What many Americans don't see is that behind much of these beliefs is an increased dabbling in the occult and a revival of ancient paganism and witchcraft. As this movement expands, we will see a steady increase in overt demonic activity in the West.

But what will the Church's response to this be? Although spiritual warfare is being discussed and taught more now than at any time this century, much of what is being taught is erroneous and unbiblical and actually results in spiritual instability instead of maturity. But I do not perceive this surge in warfare-centered teaching to be an entirely negative state of affairs. The increased attention given to this area will, I believe, be used of the Lord to

Probably the most familiar portion of Scripture from Ephesians for most believers is this passage in chapter 6. Yet very few have ever studied it in the context of the entire epistle.

move many believers to search out the Scriptures and determine what the Word really teaches about Satan and the believer's response to him. Although there is much imbalance in this arena of theology today, I fully expect this movement to mature and become more centered on the teaching of Scripture and less on subjective experience. The goal of this week's lesson is to become a partner in this process. It is not my heart's desire to throw stones at particular doctrines or people. Rather, it is my prayerful ambition to help believers shape convictions that are biblical. Even if you do not agree with all that is presented in this book, it will hopefully assist you in searching the Scriptures and drawing your own conclusions before the Lord.

I believe you are in for some surprises this week. Probably the most familiar portion of Scripture from Ephesians for most believers is this passage in chapter 6. Yet very few have ever studied it in the context of the entire epistle. As a result, many misunderstand the message and emphases of these verses. This is because Ephesians 6 is preceded by five chapters of truth that form the foundation upon which this passage rests. You may be surprised at how these verses appear after understanding what comes before them. May the Lord bless your study.

THE STRUGGLE WITH THE ENEMY (6:10—12)

We are in a spiritual war. The world, the flesh, and the devil have conspired to lead us astray from *"pure and simple devotion to Christ"* (2 Corinthians 11:3 NLT). Before addressing biblical questions regarding the practice of spiritual warfare, it is essential that we come up with a working definition of exactly what it is and what it is not. Generally speaking, spiritual warfare refers to the battle between the forces of God and the forces of Satan. The two biblical references which give this practice its name are 2 Corinthians 10:4, which says, *"for the weapons of our* **warfare** *are not of the flesh, but divinely powerful for the destruction of fortresses,"* and Ephesians 6:12 which says, *"our struggle is not against flesh and blood, but against the rulers, against the powers, against the world forces of this darkness, against the* **spiritual** *forces of wickedness in the heavenly places."* The real question of debate in the body of Christ today isn't centered on whether or not spiritual warfare is a legitimate practice, for it is clear from the Word that there is a war or struggle taking place between the forces of good and evil. The real question isn't if spiritual warfare exists, but what are its priorities and parameters. What we find being practiced in parts of the body today far exceeds the parameters the Scriptures relate and gives the practice much more priority than is biblically modeled or seems logically prudent. And yet, there is the danger of reacting to that and dismissing the subject altogether, or not speaking about it out of fear of being misunderstood. Both extremes are wrong. The goal is not to go to extremes but to move toward balance, and understanding what the Word teaches is crucial to finding that balance. A right view of Ephesians chapter 6, in the context of the epistle as a whole, will go a long way toward giving us that balance.

📖 Take a moment to read Ephesians 6:10–20. What do you think is the significance of this being the final subject Paul addresses?

_____

_____

_____

_____

_____

Throughout these final three chapters, Paul has become progressively more specific and practical, and it seems he has saved the best for last with this discussion of warfare. The ultimate application of our position in Christ is to be a soldier in His service, waging war against His enemies.

Now reread Ephesians 6:10. What does it mean to be strong in *"the strength of His might"*?

_____

_____

_____

_____

Paul seems to be emphasizing the necessity of walking in God's strength and not our own. Self-sufficiency in spiritual struggle is spiritual suicide. There is no way we can be victorious over Satan in our own strength. If we could, there would be no need for Christ.

📖 Take a look at Ephesians 6:11. What do you think it means to "put on" the full armor of God?

_____

_____

_____

_____

The Greek word translated "put on" here is *enduo* (from which our English word "endue" is derived). This same Greek word is translated "clothe" elsewhere in Scripture (such as 2 Corinthians 5:2), and here in Ephesians, it is used metaphorically. The *"armor of God"* is put on as an act of the will, like clothing. In the context of Ephesians, Christ is the armor. When we put on Christ, we put on the armor.

📖 Compare Ephesians 6:10–11 with 2 Corinthians 2:11 and write your observations on what the *"schemes"* of the devil are.

_____

_____

_____

_____

_____

> ## "Finally, be strong in the Lord and in the strength of His might."
>
> ### Ephesians 6:10

The Greek word *methodeía,* translated "schemes" in verse 11 could also be translated "craftiness." It literally means "craft, deceit, a cunning device." 2 Corinthians 2:11 warns that part of giving opportunity to Satan comes through being ignorant of his schemes. Although Satan works in many ways, his primary efforts are wrapped up in deception (various temptations) and destruction (accusations and attacks).

📖 Look at Ephesians 6:12. Why do you think it is important to acknowledge that our struggle is not against flesh and blood?

_____

_____

_____

_____

Since our struggle is not against flesh and blood, we must recognize that people are never the enemy—they are only victims of the enemy. God loves the world (its inhabitants) so much that He sent His only Son to die that mankind might be reconciled to Him. It is my perception that those who rebel the strongest are more apt to respond to the Lord than those who sit in silent apathy.

What do you think is the significance of the different enemies mentioned in verse 12?

_____

_____

_____

_____

Satan is not alone in his war against us. Scripture (see Revelation 12) suggests that one third of the angels joined Satan in his fall. Satan is called the *"prince of demons"* (Matthew 12:24 NIV), and apparently from this verse, he has them well organized in rank.

THE SECURITY IN CHRIST (6:13—15)

Satan is a lion on a leash. It is God who is preeminent. He was, is, and always will be in control. Because He is **omnipotent** (all-powerful), **omniscient** (all-knowing), and **omnipresent** (ever-present), Satan is under His authority. We see from looking at the book of Job that Satan reports to God (see Job 1:6; 2:1). And we discover there that God set the boundaries of Satan's attacks on Job (see Job 1:12, 2:6). Satan can only go as far as God allows him to go. So, why does God allow Satan to go anywhere at all? If He has the power to get rid of him, why doesn't He go ahead and do it? Have you ever considered that? Scripture doesn't attempt to give us an answer to that question; it only assures us that God's purposes are always right and for our benefit. We must remind ourselves that because God is omniscient (all-knowing), He knew before He created Satan that he would rebel. Satan would never have been created if his rebellion did not fit in

God's purposes. And when that purpose is complete, God will speak the word, and Revelation 20:1 tells us that all it takes to throw Satan into the abyss is one angel. It is a great comfort to realize that because the Lord is preeminent, He is able to use Satan's actions for our benefit and His glory. It is also a tremendous comfort to recognize that *"greater is He who is in you than he who is in the world"* (1 John 4:4). Today, we want to focus on the protection we have in Christ.

📖 Read Ephesians 6:13. What according to the text is the purpose of taking up the *"full armor of God"*?

_____

_____

_____

We are called to take up the full armor of God that we might *"stand firm"* against the schemes of the devil. It is only in Christ that we are able to be secure against Satan's onslaughts. Spiritual warfare is not about chasing the devil, but all about holding our ground against the devil. God will deal with Satan in His own time and way.

Look again at Ephesians 6:13. What do you think is the "everything" done to stand firm?

_____

_____

_____

_____

There are two dimensions mentioned here, both of which are essential to standing firm. First, the process of "putting on" our spiritual armor is detailed at length in these verses to give us an idea of the specifics of our protection. As we said before, when we put on the new garment (Christ), we have the necessary armor. The other dimension is far less obvious. It is hinted at in verse 12—the implied reality that although we *"wrestle not"* with flesh and blood, we do wrestle with Satan and his demonic forces.

📖 Most Bibles will have certain phrases from this passage in all capital letters. This means they are quoted from the Old Testament. If your Bible has a "cross-reference" feature, look at Ephesians 6:14–17 and the cross-references to see where these quotations come from. Look up these references and record your thoughts on what each cross-referenced passage means.

_____

_____

_____

_____

_____

_____

_____

_____

"You are from God, little children, and have overcome them; because greater is He who is in you than he who is in the world."

I John 4:4

As we do a thorough exegesis of this passage we find that all the armor mentioned here appears in Isaiah (see Isaiah 11:4–5; 49:2; 51:7; 59:17), where it is identified as being true of Messiah. So in a very tangible sense, when we put on Christ, we put on the armor. Positionally, our vital organs are protected when we are in Christ.

📖 The quotations in verse 14 come from Isaiah 11:5 and 59:17. Look them up in their context and write what you learn.

_____

_____

_____

_____

_____

Both of these quotations are given in the context of descriptions of Messiah. Since these are true of Messiah, it is logical that they would be true of us positionally (since we are "in Him"), and they would also be true of us practically as we yield control of our lives to Him by being "filled" with the Spirit. Almost every aspect of the armor is mentioned in Isaiah and is thereby linked with Christ, the Messiah.

Ephesians 6 introduces the believer to his protection in Christ, called the "armor" of God. In addressing the armor, several factors must be established. First and foremost, where does our armor come from? It is the armor *"of God."* A key truth to recognize is that the believer's defense does not begin with the believer; it begins with God. All that God is . . . is all that we need. And all that He is comes to our aid in this arena of spiritual warfare. God the Father, God the Son, and God the Holy Spirit are all involved in our defense. Psalm 28:8 puts it this way: *"The Lord is their strength, and He is a saving defense to His anointed."*

THE SECURITY IN CHRIST (CONTINUED)

You and I are secure in Christ. According to Ephesians 6, these essential pieces of protection (the girded loins, the breastplate of righteousness, the shod feet) are permanently in place at salvation. If Christ is my righteousness, how is it possible for me to remove my righteousness? If Christ is my righteousness and He will neither leave me nor forsake me (see Hebrews 13:5), then my vital organs are always protected. Likewise, my salvation, which is my helmet, protects my head from fatal blows. There is an interesting change of pattern when we get to verse 17. Rather than using the same word he used in verse 16 for "taking" up the shield of faith (*analambáno*), Paul uses a different word to "take" the helmet of salvation (*déchomai*), which literally means "receive." Again, "If salvation is our helmet, how can we take it off?" It is my opinion that the essential aspects of my protection are in place when I clothe myself with Christ. An important part of the believer's defense is the fact that he is in Christ.

📖 Read Ephesians 6:14. What do you think it means to "gird your loins" with truth?

_____

_____

_____

_____

To gird our loins with truth would be to prepare ourselves for battle with truth. Truth guards us against stumbling, frees us up to move, and prepares us for war with the enemy.

Look over Ephesians 6:14 again. What do you think is the significance of having righteousness as a breastplate?

_____

_____

_____

_____

Christ's righteousness, which is ours positionally because we are "in Him," is identified as our breastplate. This is significant because a breastplate when accompanied by a helmet covers and protects all vital organs. The implication is obvious. When we surround ourselves with Christ's righteousness and take salvation as a helmet (both of which occurred positionally when we met Christ), we are secure against Satan's attacks. He may knock us off our feet or injure us or hinder our effectiveness, but he cannot inflict a fatal wound.

📖 The quotation in verse 15 is found in Isaiah 52:7. Look at it in its context and see what light it sheds on this verse.

_____

_____

_____

_____

_____

📖 Isaiah 52:7 appears in the context of God's comfort to Israel. The good news must first be given to us, but it must also be given through us. This is God's desire.

Reflect on Ephesians 6:15 and answer the questions below.

_____

_____

_____

_____

Did You Know?
GIRD YOUR LOINS

The phrase, "gird up your loins," comes from military language of the day. Roman soldiers wore at least one of several wide belts or girdles as part of their uniform. The breech-like leather apron protected the lower abdomen, and the sword-belt was buckled on with the sword. Usually both were put on just before battle. Additionally, sometimes soldiers would prepare for battle by tucking the ends of their robes in their belt so that they would not trip over them.

What do you think it means to have your feet shod with the preparation of the gospel of peace?

_____

_____

_____

_____

When does this occur?

_____

_____

This verse is translated in the past tense because our feet were fitted with *"the readiness to announce the Good News of peace"* (Ephesians 6:15 TEV) when we first experienced God's salvation. From the very moment of spiritual birth, we were mobilized into God's army, and our feet were shod with the gospel of peace. (The word "gospel" means "good news" and the peace spoken of is peace with God.) If we understood enough truth to be saved, we understand enough to help someone else receive salvation.

If you miss everything else, you must get this one central point—we already have the armor because we have Jesus. We need to be strong in His strength, not our own, and we need to be sure that we are Spirit-filled and He is in control. But we needn't fear what the devil can do. He is not greater than Jesus. We are secure in Him.

THE STRATEGY OF THE BELIEVER (6:16—24)

As we saw in Day Two and Day Three, we as Christians are protected in Christ. Because we are in Him, our vital organs are covered. What is lacking to complete our armor (*"full armor"*) is for us to take up the shield, which we do by walking in the faith, and making use of the sword, the "word" (*rhēma*) of God, which probably refers to the individual Scripture spoken to us by the Spirit in our time of need. When Paul speaks of the *"shield of faith,"* the word "faith" appears in the Greek with the definite article. This means he is referring not to faith in general (the principle of faith), but to a specific faith ("the faith"). Usually when the word "faith" is structured this way, it refers to the tenets of the Christian faith and is synonymous with walking with God in sound doctrine. In addition, we do battle when we pray. The context of verses 18–20 indicates that these verses are also related to the subject of spiritual warfare. It is also worth mentioning that we see no case in this passage for the prospect of warfare being a battle fought internally. Satan cannot possess a believer because the believer is already possessed by Christ.

📖 Look over Ephesians 6:16. In what way do you think faith is a shield?

_____

_____

_____

_____

Did You Know?
FLAMING ARROWS

Flaming arrows (see Ephesians 6:16) in biblical times, were hollowed reeds filled with flammable liquid that would explode on impact and had to be extinguished. They were comparable to the modern "Molotov Cocktail."

Proverbs 30:5 says *"Every word of God is tested; He is a shield to those who take refuge in Him."* Faith is nothing special other than the fact that it is placed in a faithful God. God is our shield and faith is His ordained vehicle to bring this into our experience.

📖 The quotation in verse 17 is from Isaiah 59:17. Look at it in its context and write what is relevant here.

_____

_____

_____

_____

Word Study
"EVIL ONE"

The "evil one" spoken of here in Ephesians 6:16 (literally "the evil") is obviously Satan. Of the two Greek words translated evil, *kakós* (inherent evil) and *ponērós* (evil which seeks to draw in others), the latter is used here.

Like the other quotes from Isaiah, this one also is in the context of a description of Messiah. This passage tells us that we must "take" (literally "receive" [from a different word than the one translated "take" in verse 16]) salvation. The emphasis seems to be on the point of initiating salvation (justification), which for them was past tense, rather than the process of salvation (sanctification).

📖 The last half of Ephesians 6:17 is probably a reference to Isaiah 49:2. Compare this with Hebrews 4:12 and write your observations.

_____

_____

_____

_____

In Isaiah 49:2, the Messiah is described as having a mouth *"like a sharp sword."* In Hebrews 4:12, Isaiah's prophetic description is clarified as being the allegoric description of God's words. In the context of Ephesians 6, the concept takes on a more militant meaning as we view the Word of God as a key offensive weapon in our arsenal against Satan's army. The other aspect of our offense mentioned here is prayer. When Jesus encountered Satan in the wilderness (see Matthew 4) He employed both prayer and the Word of God. (Prayer is implied with Christ's fasting.)

📖 Examine Ephesians 6:18. What do you think it means to *"pray at all times in the Spirit"*?

_____

_____

_____

_____

Did You Know?

"ALL"–POWERFUL PRAYER

In this brief section on prayer (Ephesians 6:18), the apostle Paul uses the word "all" four different times, setting some good parameters for praying. *"With all prayer,"* we are to *"pray at all times in the Spirit."* We are to be on the alert *"with all perseverance,"* and to make *"petition for all the saints."*

Basically it means being "Spirit-filled" (5:18) while praying—your spirit communicating with God. If we are honest with ourselves, we have to admit that often our praying isn't communicating with God, but with ourselves or those around us. True prayer is our spirit communicating with God's Spirit (see John 4:24). Prayer isn't prayer unless this communication happens.

📖 Read Ephesians 6:19–20. How do these verses fit with verse 18?

_____

_____

_____

_____

_____

Verse 18 describes the offensive weapon of prayer and is Paul's exhortation to the Ephesians to make use of this effective weapon. Verses 19 and 20 provide an immediate opportunity for them to apply it in aid of Paul. He has told them to *"be on the alert with all perseverance and petition for all the saints."* Certainly, Paul is a saint in need of their petitions.

An important issue to bring up at this point is that there is no biblical substantiation for "praying on the armor" piece by piece, though some may try to put on the armor in this way. In a very practical sense, we put the armor on when we put on Christ (yield ourselves to His control and lordship in every area of our lives). Paul differentiates the aspects of the armor as a metaphor here to help the Ephesians (and all believers) visualize their protection in Christ. We do a real disservice to Ephesians 6 when we separate it from the rest of Ephesians, yet few of us have really taken the time to understand the chapter in the context of the entire epistle. The central theme of the entire book of Ephesians is who we are in Christ. Chapter 6, viewed in this light, is not presenting a series of disjointed truths, but presents one truth: Christ. Because of this reality, I do not believe that the armor should be viewed as individual pieces, but as the parts of a whole.

Paul closes out this wonderful book with some personal notes. In verses 21–22, Paul speaks of sending Tychicus to them to personally update them on his imprisonment for the cause of Christ. This reveals the personal love which must have existed between Paul and this church he helped to found. In his closing words he wishes them peace, love with faith, and grace. Make Paul's final comments in Ephesians your prayer both for yourself and for those that you love in Christ.

Ephesians 6:10-24

FOR ME TO FOLLOW GOD

Sooner or later, every believer discovers that the Christian life is a battleground, not a playground, and that he faces an enemy who is much stronger than he is (apart form the Lord). Though we often get deceived into thinking otherwise, *"our struggle is **not** against flesh and blood"* (Ephesians 6:12). People are not the enemy, they're victims of the enemy. A spiritual battle is going on in this world and in the sphere of the "heavenly places," and you and I are a part of this battle. Knowing this makes "walking in victory" a vitally important thing to us—and to God. It is essential that we as believers understand that Jesus, by His death and resurrection, overcame the world (see John 16:33; Galatians 6:14), the flesh (see Galatians 2:20; Romans 6:1–6), and the devil (see Ephesians 1:19–23). In other words, as believers, we do not fight **for** victory—we fight **from** victory! The Spirit of God enables us, by faith, to appropriate Christ's victory for ourselves. These questions should help in the process.

Do you usually approach life with an awareness of the spiritual battle?

_____

_____

_____

How can you be more effective in this area?

_____

_____

_____

_____

We must remember the "schemes" or strategies of our enemy. Sometimes his attack is a frontal assault. Other times it is deceptively hidden. Sometimes he appears as an angel of light. One effective scheme of the enemy is to try to make us forget that we are in a spiritual battle—to lull us to sleep. We must be on the alert—we must stay awake!

When you are in spiritual struggle do you tend to rely on your own strength or the Lord's?

_____

_____

_____

_____

We saw in this passage that we are to gird our loins with truth in preparation for battle. Truth frees your movement and keeps you from stumbling. Is study of God's truth (Scripture) enough of a priority in your life?

_____

_____

_____

_____

What changes do you need to make in this area?

_____

_____

_____

_____

_____

"Our struggle is __not__ against flesh and blood" (Ephesians 6:12). People are not the enemy, they're victims of the enemy.

TRUSTING GOD IN THE HEAT OF BATTLE

Hebrews 11:6 says, *"And without faith it is impossible to please Him, for he who comes to God must believe that He is and that He is a rewarder of those who seek Him."* If we want to be pleasing to the Lord, we are going to have to trust Him, especially in battles of the spiritual realm.

Paul exhorts us to *"take up the shield of faith."* The term "faith" (*pístis*) is used in two different ways in the New Testament. It is used of trust—our choice to trust God with a situation or circumstance. It is also used of the whole of what we believe. We follow the Christian faith—the doctrines of truth laid down by the apostles. It is likely that both concepts of this word "faith" are woven into this idea of the shield. While doctrine is related to truth—what we just looked at, we must also see our shield as our trust in truth. Hebrews 11:6 says, *"And without faith it is impossible to please Him, for he who comes to God must believe that He is and that He is a rewarder of those who seek Him."* If we want to be pleasing to the Lord, we are going to have to trust Him, especially in battles of the spiritual realm.

Is your Christian life healthy or stagnant in the area of walking by faith?

_____

_____

_____

_____

What are some steps of faith God would have you make in your present situation?

_____

_____

_____

_____

_____

Prayer is the spiritual lifeblood of the believer. What changes in this area need to be made as a result of this message?

_____

_____

_____

Why not close this lesson and this study with an application of Ephesians 6:18. Use the space below to write out your prayer to the Lord, putting into action the four "alls" of prayer.

_____

_____

_____

_____

_____

_____

_____

_____

Notes

Notes

How to
Follow God

Starting the Journey

Did you know that you have been on God's heart and mind for a long, long time? Even before time existed you were on His mind. He has always wanted you to know Him in a personal, purposeful relationship. He has a purpose for your life and it is founded upon His great love for you. You can be assured it is a good purpose and it lasts forever. Our time on this earth is only the beginning. God has a grand design that goes back into eternity past and reaches into eternity future. What is that design?

The Scriptures are clear about God's design for man—God created man to live and walk in oneness with Himself. Oneness with God means being in a relationship that is totally unselfish, totally satisfying, totally secure, righteous and pure in every way. That's what we were created for. If we walked in that kind of relationship with God we would glorify Him and bring pleasure to Him. Life would be right! Man was meant to live that way—pleasing to God and glorifying Him (giving a true estimate of who God is). Adam sinned and shattered his oneness with God. Ever since, man has come short of the glory of God: man does not and cannot please God or give a true estimate of God. Life is not right until a person is right with God. That is very clear as we look at the many people who walked across the pages of Scripture, both Old and New Testaments.

JESUS CHRIST came as the solution for this dilemma. Jesus Christ is the glory of God—the true estimate of who God is in every way. He pleased His Father in everything He did and said, and He came to restore oneness with God. He came to give man His power and grace to walk in oneness with God, to follow Him day by day enjoying the relationship for which he was created. In the process, man could begin to present a true picture of Who God is and experience knowing Him personally. You may be asking, "How do these facts impact my life today? How does this become real to me now? How can I begin the journey of following God in this way?" To come to know God personally means you must choose to receive Jesus Christ as your personal Savior and Lord.

- First of all, you must admit that you have sinned, that you are not walking in oneness with God, not pleasing Him or glorifying Him in your life (Romans 3:23; 6:23; 8:5-8).
- It means repenting of that sin—changing your mind, turning to God and turning away from sin—and by faith receiving His forgiveness based on His death on the Cross for you (Romans 3:21-26; 1 Peter 3:18).
- It means opening your life to receive Him as your living, resurrected Lord and Savior (John 1:12). He has promised to come and indwell you by His Spirit and live in you as the Savior and Master of your life (John 14:16-21; Romans 14:7-9).
- He wants to live His life through you—conforming you to His image, bearing His fruit through you and giving you power to reign in life (John 15:1,4-8; Romans 5:17; 7:4; 8:29, 37).

You can come to Him now. In your own words, simply tell Him you want to know Him personally and you willingly repent of your sin and receive His forgiveness and His life. Tell Him you want to follow Him forever (Romans 10:9-10, 13). Welcome to the Family of God and to the greatest journey of all!!!

Walking on the Journey

How do we follow Him day by day? Remember, Christ has given those who believe in Him everything pertaining to life and godliness, so that we no longer have to be slaves to our "flesh" and its corruption (2 Peter 1:3-4). Day by day He wants to empower us to live a life of love and joy, pleasing to Him and rewarding to us. That's why Ephesians 5:18 tells us to "*be filled with the Spirit*"—keep on being controlled by the Spirit who lives in you. He knows exactly what we need each day and we can trust Him to lead us (Proverbs 3:5-6). So how can we cooperate with Him in this journey together?

To walk with Him *day by day* means ...
- reading and listening to His Word day by day (Luke 10:39, 42; Colossians 3:16; Psalm 19:7-14; 119:9).
- spending time talking to Him in prayer (Philippians 4:6-7).
- realizing that God is God and you are not, and the role that means He has in your life.

This allows Him to work through your life as you fellowship, worship, pray and learn with other believers (Acts 2:42), and serve in the good works He has prepared for us to do—telling others who Jesus is and what His Word says, teaching and encouraging others, giving to help meet needs, helping others, etc. (Ephesians 2:10).

God's goal for each of us is that we be conformed to the image of His Son, Jesus Christ (Romans 8:29). But none of us will reach that goal of perfection until we are with Him in Heaven, for then "we shall be like Him, because we shall see Him just as He is" (1 John 3:2). For now, He wants us to follow

Him faithfully, learning more each day. Every turn in the road, every trial and every blessing, is designed to bring us to a new depth of surrender to the Lord and His ways. He not only wants us to do His will, He desires that we surrender to His will His way. That takes trust—trust in His character, His plan and His goals (Proverbs 3:5-6).

As you continue this journey, and perhaps you've been following Him for a while, you must continue to listen carefully and follow closely. We never graduate from that. That sensitivity to God takes moment by moment surrender, dying to the impulses of our flesh to go our own way, saying no to the temptations of Satan to doubt God and His Word, and refusing the lures of the world to be unfaithful to the Lord who gave His life for us.

God desires that each of us come to maturity as sons and daughters: to that point where we are fully satisfied in Him and His ways, fully secure in His sovereign love, and walking in the full measure of His purity and holiness. If we are to clearly present the image of Christ for all to see, it will take daily surrender and daily seeking to follow Him wherever He leads, however He gets there (Luke 9:23-25). It's a faithful walk of trust through time into eternity. And it is worth everything. Trust Him. Listen carefully. Follow closely.

The *Following God*
Bible Character Study Series

Life Principles from the Old Testament

Characters include: Adam, Noah, Job, Abraham, Lot, Jacob, Joseph, Moses, Caleb, Joshua, Gideon, and Samson
ISBN 0-89957-300-2   208 pages

Life Principles from the Kings of the Old Testament

Characters include: Saul, David, Solomon, Jereboam I, Asa, Ahab, Jehoshaphat, Hezekiah, Josiah, Zerubbabel & Ezra, Nehemiah, and "The True King in Israel."
ISBN 0-89957-301-0   256 pages

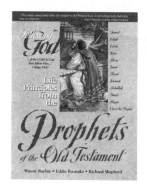

Life Principles from the Prophets of the Old Testament

Characters include: Samuel, Elijah, Elisha, Jonah, Hosea, Isaiah, Micah, Jeremiah, Habakkuk, Daniel, Haggai, and "Christ the Prophet."
ISBN 0-89957-303-7   224 pages

Leader's Guides for Following God™ books are available.
To order now, call (800) 266-4977 or (423) 894-6060.
Or order online at www.amgpublishers.com

The *Following God*
Bible Character Study Series

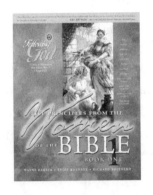

Life Principles from the Women of the Bible (Book One)

Characters include: Eve, Sarah, Miriam, Rahab, Deborah, Ruth, Hannah, Esther, The Virtuous Woman, Mary & Martha, Mary, the Mother of Jesus, and "The Bride of Christ."
ISBN 0-89957-302-9   224 pages

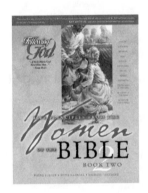

Life Principles from the Women of the Bible (Book Two)

Characters include: Hagar, Lot's Wife, Rebekah, Leah, Rachel, Abigail, Bathsheba, Jezebel, Elizabeth, The Woman at the Well, Women of the Gospels, and "The Submissive Wife."
ISBN 0-89957-308-8   224 pages

Life Principles from the New Testament Men of Faith

Characters include: John the Baptist, Peter, John, Thomas, James, Barnabas, Paul, Paul's Companions, Timothy, and "The Son of Man."
ISBN 0-89957-304-5   208 pages

Call for more information (800) 266-4977 or (423) 894-6060.
Or order online at www.amgpublishers.com

Following God™ Discipleship Series

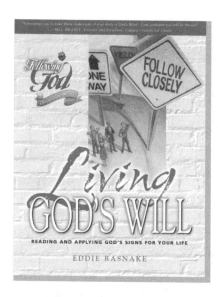

Living God's Will

ISBN 0-89957-309-6

How can I follow and identify the signs that lead to God's will? *Living God's Will* explores the answer to this all-important question in detail. It is Eddie Rasnake's deeply-held conviction that the road to God's will is well-marked with signposts to direct us. Each lesson in this twelve-week Bible study takes a look at a different signpost that reflects God's will. You will be challenged to recognize the signposts of God when you encounter them. But more importantly, you will be challenged to follow God's leading by following the direction of those signposts.

In the pages of this "Following God" study on finding and obeying God's will, you will find clear and practical advice for:

✓ Yielding your life to the Lord

✓ Recognizing God's will through Scripture, prayer and circumstances

✓ Seeking godly counsel

✓ Discovering how God's peace enters into the process of following His will

✓ Determining God's will in areas not specifically addressed in Scripture, such as choosing a wife/husband or career path.

Throughout your study you will also be enriched by the many interactive application sections that literally thousands have come to appreciate from the acclaimed **Following God** series.

To order, call (800) 266-4977 or (423) 894-6060
www.amgpublishers.com

Other Discipleship Series books now available.
Watch for new Following God™ titles to be released soon!

Following God™ Discipleship Series

First Steps for the New Christian

ISBN 0-89957-311-8

I'm new to this. I didn't even know I was in a race. The Bible likens the Christian life to a marathon. The apostle Paul said, *Run in such a way that you may win."* **Following God™—** *First Steps for the New Christian* will help you start out on the right foot and stay there with practical studies designed to get new runners in shape to finish the race.

In the pages of this book, you will find clear and practical advice that answers the following questions:

✓ What is your position in Christ?

✓ What is spiritual growth and what is not spiritual growth?

✓ How should a Christian deal with sin?

✓ How important are Bible study, prayer, and meditation to the Christian walk?

✓ What should Christians do to cultivate the gifts, talents, and opportunites that God gives them?

Throughout your study you will also be enriched by the many interactive application sections that literally thousands have come to appreciate from the acclaimed **Following God** series.

To order, call (800) 266-4977 or (423) 894-6060
www.amgpublishers.com

Other Discipleship Series books now available.
Watch for new Following God™ titles to be released soon!

Notes

Notes

Notes